S0-BDR-927

I am Already Successful

80 Activities to Develop Motivation and Self-Esteem

by Dennis Hooker

I Am *Already* Succcessful
80 Activities to Develop Motivation and Self-Esteem

©1998 by JIST Works, Inc.

Published by JIST Works, Inc.
720 N. Park Avenue
Indianapolis, IN 46202-3490
Phone: 317-264-3720 Fax: 317-264-3709 E-mail: jistworks@aol.com
World Wide Web Address: http://www.jist.com

Other Books by Dennis Hooker
I Can Manage Life

See the back of this book for additional JIST titles and ordering information. Quantity discounts are available.

Interior Design by Debbie Berman
Cover Design by Honeymoon Image & Design

Printed in the United States of America

1 2 3 4 5 6 7 8 9   02 01 00 99 98 97

All rights reserved. No part of this book may be reproduced in any form or by any means, or stored in a database or retrieval system, without prior permission of the publisher except in case of brief quotations embodied in articles or reviews. Making copies of any part of this book for any purpose other than your own personal use is a violation of United States copyright laws.

We have been careful to provide accurate information throughout this book, but it is possible that errors and omissions have been introduced. Please consider this in making any career plans or other important decisions. Trust your own judgment above all else and in all things.

ISBN: 1-56370-425-0

Contents

Introduction 1

What Makes This Book Unique? 1
How This Book Is Organized 2
Being Successful Through Simulations 3
Moving On to Success 4

Section 1

You Are Unique 5

Activity 1. Opinions 6
Activity 2. Time Capsule 8
Activity 3. I Like to 10
Activity 4. The Perfect Person 12
Activity 5. Language 14
Activity 6. As I See It 16
Activity 7. Daydreaming 18
Activity 8. Motivation 20
Activity 9. The Describe-It Game 22
Activity 10. A Place for Everything 24
Activity 11. There's Only One You 26
Activity 12. Think-Tank Products 28
Activity 13. Make a "Somethink" 31
Activity 14. How I See You 33
Activity 15. Levels of Importance 35
Activity 16. Successfully Unique 38
Activity 17. A Successful Person 40
Activity 18. Ways I Am Already Successful 42
Activity 19. Seeds of Service 1 44
Activity 20. Planning and Scheduling 46
Activity 21. Needs 48
Activity 22. Feelings Defined 50
Activity 23. Discarded Computer Parts 53
Activity 24. My Problem 55
Activity 25. Contracting 57
Activity 26. Buried Talents 59
Activity 27. Intelligence 62
Activity 28. It's Your Choice 64
Activity 29. Do You Agree? 66
Activity 30. Test Me 68
Simulation 1. *The Game* 70
Evaluation of *The Game* 71

Small Group Inventory 1 72
Self-Inventory 1 74
Moving On 75

Section 2
Success with Others 77

Activity 31. Interviewing Techniques 78
Activity 32. Planning a Job Interview 81
Activity 33. Interviewing 83
Activity 34. Working Together 85
Activity 35. Cooperation 87
Activity 36. Good "Followership" 89
Activity 37. You're the Boss 91
Activity 38. Team Evaluation of Prospective Employees 94
Activity 39. Discussions and Debates 97
Activity 40. Vote on It 99
Activity 41. Be an Expert 102
Activity 42. Evaluating Experts 104
Activity 43. The Decision-Making Process 106
Activity 44. Live Life or Be Run by It 108
Activity 45. Remembering 110
Activity 46. Your Classmates 112
Activity 47. Using Graphic Words 114
Activity 48. Feelings List 116
Activity 49. Feelings Bingo 119
Activity 50. The Sponge 121
Activity 51. Working with Others: Seeds of Service 2 123
Simulation 2. *The Business* 125
Small Group Inventory 2 126
Self-Inventory 2 127
Moving On 129

Section 3
Your Success in the World 131

Activity 52. Design Your Own Evaluation 132
Activity 53. Sharing Your Interests 134
Activity 54. Unwritten Words 136
Activity 55. The Courtroom 138
Activity 56. Two Sides to an Argument 140
Activity 57. Learning Modes 142
Activity 58. Body Talk 144
Activity 59. Present Your Viewpoint 146
Activity 60. Compare with High Standard 148
Activity 61. My Place 150

Activity 62. Curiosity 152
Activity 63. Cliff-Hangers 154
Activity 64. You Decide 156
Activity 65. What Did People Do Before Reading? 158
Activity 66. Roots 160
Activity 67. Find Blends 162
Activity 68. Simplify the Complex 164
Activity 69. Complicate the Simple 166
Activity 70. Illusions 168
Activity 71. Technical Writing 170
Activity 72. Alike and Different 173
Activity 73. Your Page 175
Activity 74. Thoughts and Feelings 176
Activity 75. Who You Were 178
Activity 76. Who You Are 180
Activity 77. Who You Will Be 182
Activity 78. You Were, Are, and Will Be … 184
Activity 79. Seeds of Service 3 186
Activity 80. Time Capsule Revisited 188
Simulation 3. *The Communiqué* 189
Small Group Inventory 3 191
Self-Inventory 3 192
You Are Successful: Some Final Thoughts 194

Introduction

Imagine that a friend has just said to you, "Someday, I am going to be successful." This puzzles you because you thought your friend was already successful. Your friend is doing well, has a good attitude, and enjoys a sense of personal accomplishment. Is it possible that your friend cannot accept that he or she is already successful?

The world around us seems to tell us that success is something we *achieve*, a triumph or a victory. We are led to believe that "success" is an accomplishment of conquerors and champions. These conquerors are "successful." The victorious leave behind victims.

But, *success* can have a more satisfying meaning. Success can mean enjoying your present status—which means liking and accepting your present state of mind. It is saying to yourself, "I am *already* successful. I do not have to do anything different. I do not have to wait for some accomplishment in the future to feel successful."

As you complete the activities in this book, you will experience this more realistic attitude by learning that you *are* already successful. Of course, there is room in your life and in your thinking for improvement, but success is already yours. This is not a positive-thinking pep talk; it is a fact.

Remember, your working definition of "success" is to enjoy making the journey, not something you achieve after you arrive at your destination. You are successful when you accept your success. Success does not depend on the quality of the project or the evaluation of others. When you accept your success, you can say, "I am already successful because I am a worthwhile person and accept my own worth!"

What Makes This Book Unique?

I Am Already Successful is *by you*—and *about you*. This book is unique because it has no "right" or "wrong" answers. Nothing that you answer can be marked off! *You* will decide how much energy you invest in these experiences. Other members of your work group will help you by sharing their experiences with you and by letting you share your experiences with them.

In this book, you will discover what you like, how you feel, how you see others, and how they see you. You will feel successful every step of the way.

As you answer the questions on the following pages, you will begin to see this as more than a simple book of worksheets. The responses you make map a journey through your own experiences. And, as the author, I am your guide. I can show you some points of interest, but it is up to you to enjoy the trip.

Before we begin, however, I have some clear-cut goals for the journey I want to share, so that you know where we are going:

1. You will discover that *you are already successful*. You do not have to become something or somebody else to be a success.

2. The way you appear to others typically is how you *think* you are. In this book, you will learn how to let others see that you are successful.

3. You will discover that you can prosper without "being better" than someone else. Cooperation is better than competition. (If you feel competitive, try self-improvement—doing something better than you used to.)

4. You will acquire *an attitude* of being already successful. You will probably "catch it" before you actually realize it.

5. When you feel successful, you can help those around you. You will find enjoyment, satisfaction, and personal growth using what you have right now to help others. What you do in the future will demonstrate your interest in other people.

After you finish the exercises in this book, you will be able to express your opinion without worrying about whether it is accepted or not. *Your opinion is yours*. Working alone and as a member of small groups, you will complete several projects. What you gain from these projects will be more rewarding than mere grades and applause.

I call these small groups "think tanks." The term describes a group in which people put their heads together and solve problems or discuss issues.

The projects in this book are tasks that you work on alone first, then share with others in your small groups. The results of many of these projects are then reported to the whole class. After you come up with your own ideas, you coordinate your decision with others in your small group. Later, your group will help you explain or justify your decision to the total group.

How This Book Is Organized

Each activity in *I Am Already Successful* is arranged into the following sections:

Challenge

You read and think about a problem or a thought-provoking statement or quote.

Exercise

You work on a task alone or in a small group. These exercises typically take 15 to 30 minutes.

Putting It Together

You pull together loose ends and reflect with your small group on what you wrote in the exercise. Some of your individual and small group experiences are shared with the total group.

Being Successful Through Simulations

A simulation is an activity that gives you the feel of and practice for doing the real thing. A video game, for example, can give you some of the experience of driving a race car or flying an airplane.

In a similar way, you will be asked to do simulations of the "real world." A simulation is not artificial work. It is *real*. Thus, your tasks are real and demand the focused use of your energy.

All activities in this book lead to one of three major simulations:

▼ *The Game*

▼ *The Business*

▼ *The Communiqué*

Each simulation absorbs several concentrated hours and demands what you already know about the world and yourself. Each simulation will challenge you to work cooperatively with other members of your simulation team.

There are no passing grades or failures in a simulation. It is *not* a test. But, like most tasks, your progress is evaluated. You will judge what you have learned and how you have applied yourself. For example, if the game you create is a commercial disaster, you have discovered what the market does *not* want in a new game. You have successfully learned from an apparent "failure."

Moving On to Success

Now you are ready to explore the first of three parts of this book. Over the remainder of this book, you will be asked to give your opinions on many issues. Remember, there are no right or wrong answers here—only differences of opinion!

In the next section, you will see why you are already special—*you are already a success!*

You Are Unique

No one else is exactly like you—you are unique. You could be one of identical twins and still be unlike your twin. Part of what makes you unique is the way you express yourself. The way you think and communicate is yours alone. Only *you* have the exact tone of voice, the mannerisms, the key phrases, and the patterns of thought that are yours.

Language is your vehicle for letting others know who you are, what you like and dislike, your plans for the future, and so on. You already are successful in using the verbal and nonverbal symbols that make up language. How do I know? Because you are reading this book, which means something is working for you. In this first section, you will discover more about what you think and feel. You can increase your successes by communicating your ideas more effectively and by better understanding what others are communicating to you.

In Section 1, you will work toward the first simulation, *The Game.* As you complete the activities, you will identify opinions you already have and use your language skills to express those opinions to others. You will look at the word *success* and decide what it means *to you.*

Working in small groups, you will decide the importance of things around you. What is important enough to make you angry? What could make you change your opinions? You will begin to see how you can use your success to help those around you.

At the end of this section is the first simulation: *The Game.* In it, you will combine what you know now with what you discover in this section. After the simulation, you will decide what you liked and didn't like about your performance in the simulation. Then you will evaluate how you performed.

Activity 1.
Opinions

Challenge

"Don't bother me with the facts. My mind is already made up."

Your opinion is what you think is true. An opinion may or may not be based on fact. An opinion is what you *feel* to be right or good.

Take a few minutes and complete Exercise #1. Don't rush through the exercise: Take time to think about what you really feel strongly about.

Exercise #1

Decide if you agree or disagree with the following opinions. Circle "Yes" if you agree and "No" if you disagree. Rewrite each "No" response to make it true for you. For "Yes" responses give an example.

Choice	Opinion
☒ Yes ☐ No	There will be some classes I won't like next year.
☐ Yes ☒ No	I will always like my classmates. *I won't always like my classmates.*
☒ Yes ☐ No	The world will probably get worse before it gets better.
☒ Yes ☐ No	Some people are much better than others.
☒ Yes ☐ No	I can usually tell before I talk to new persons if I will like them.
☐ Yes ☐ No	People from some countries are easier to trust than people from other countries.

☑ Yes ☐ No   I can spot a phony person a mile away.

☐ Yes ☒ No   I seldom prejudge a person.

I ⬤ always prejudge a person

☐ Yes ☒ No   I'm sure I'll never make the same mistakes my parents made.

I might make the same "

☐ Yes ☒ No   It won't take much to make the world a better place.

It will take alot to "

Putting It Together

Divide into small groups and take turns answering the following questions. Make sure everyone gets a chance to talk.

▼ What do I really feel strongly about?

▼ What doesn't interest me?

▼ Am I used to giving my opinions?

▼ Will I be graded for an opinion?

▼ How can presenting my opinions let others know I am already successful?

▼ Do I really think I am (already) successful?

Discuss your answers to Exercise #1 with members of your group. Attempt to get others to see your point of view.

▼ Which opinion was the hardest to convince others of?

▼ Which opinion was the easiest to convince others of?

▼ Were you successful in changing anyone's mind?

Activity 2.

Time Capsule

Challenge

Your school wants you to place important information about yourself in a time capsule to be opened in 100 years. You decide to record your information on a computer disk, so you slip a blank disk into the drive, flip the switch to On, and press the Enter key.

In Exercise #2, use the space to write your information about you. Remember, this information will be read by people who have never met you, so be as clear as you can. What do you want the people of the future to know about you?

Exercise #2

Write your information about yourself on the monitor below. When you are finished, read back over your screen to see if it says what you want it to say.

Here are some questions to get you started:

I like: _my boyfriend & Driving around_

I am good at: _Driving_

Here are some things I think are important: _my family,_
friends, and my boyfriend,
Bobby.

I don't like to: _____

I believe: _____

_____

Putting It Together

In your small groups, read your screens to one another. If someone has written something on his or her screen that you don't understand, ask questions about it until you do understand it. Use your answers to others' questions to make your own screen more complete and clear.

Activity 3.
I Like to ...

Challenge

It's important (for both me and you) to know clearly what you like and dislike.

In this activity, you will think about what you like and don't like to do. Some questions about your likes and dislikes are easy to answer: For example, you either do or don't like green beans. Others are harder: For example, do you like to lead or follow? Proceed with caution or plunge right in? Your likes and dislikes say a great deal about who you are.

Exercise #3

Read through the following list of thoughts, feelings, and actions. For each one, mark whether you really like (**RL**), like (**L**), dislike (**D**), or really dislike (**RD**) the item.

RD show my feelings	L be in new places	L enjoy what is
RL patch up quarrels	L adapt to change	happening "now"
L be easy to know	RD make tough decisions	D question decisions
L be complimented	RL feel loved	L prove myself
RD speak	L sympathize	L follow a schedule
L work hard	RL be a friend	RD read books
RL have choices	L seek help	RD be criticized
L be alone	D make a statement	RD be bored
L visit museums	RL compliment someone	RD be anxious
RL point out mistakes	RL be modest	RD be in a rut
L be fair	L be deliberate	L help myself
L be orderly	L be excited	RD criticize
RL have new friends	L express myself	RL be able to see ahead
RL decide own life	L be logical	L be imaginative
RL act casual	D have surprises	RD plunge into tasks

L be superstitious
L argue
L be gentle

L help others
D be cooperative
RL feel loving

D think
D discuss
D study

RL plan my future
L fix broken objects
L notice strangers

L make plans
RD get annoyed
L be careful

RL be a boss
D be scared
RL be confident
RD be surprised

RL party
RD have emergencies
D create

L cause trouble
L act impulsively
RD make mistakes

L enjoy the unexpected
D respect rights
L like sunny days

L be merciful
RD write
L feel attractive

L be open to suggestions
D act detached
DD see rainy days

L enjoy thrill rides
L keep secrets
RD see rainy days
L act confident

L meet new people
L tolerate others
L be a follower

RD be expressive
L bring happiness
L be embarrassed

RD worry
L be in crowds
D read quickly

L go to movies
L have common sense
L be literate

RL be helped
L be intimate
L be spiritual

L show leadership
RL travel
L have hobbies
L enjoy modern art

Putting It Together

In your small groups, take turns answering the following questions.

▼ Do the answers I gave on Exercise #3 show any obvious patterns about my likes and dislikes? If so, what are they?

▼ What surprises me?

▼ What is not a surprise at all?

Activity 4.
The Perfect Person

Challenge

All people have an ideal—an image in their heads of the perfect person. What characteristics make up the perfect person for you?

We frequently change our "heroes" as we grow and learn new things. The superheroes of childhood give way to new role models—people we admire for their talents, their achievements, or their characteristics. Sometimes what we admire in others is what we want to acquire for ourselves. In Exercise #4, you will describe your "perfect person." Remember, there are no "right" or "wrong" answers in this exercise.

Exercise #4

In the spaces below, write your answers to the questions.

What does the perfect person look like?

5⁸, blue eyes, blonde hair, well dressed

How does the perfect person act with loved ones?

loving, funny, nice

How does the perfect person act around friends and classmates?

funny, 1 the same way.

What does the perfect person believe?

What are the advantages and disadvantages of having a perfect person as an ideal?

the advantage would be they're perfect But the disadvantage would be they could be anoyingly perfect.

In what ways am I similar to this perfect person?

_____

_____

In what ways do I differ from this perfect person?

_____

_____

Putting It Together

Describe your ideal person to others in your group. Then take turns answering these questions:

▼ How do your ideas of "perfect" qualities differ from others' in your group?

▼ How are they the same?

Work with your group to design *the* perfect person. Be very specific. You can make a list or a narrative—such as "A Day in the Life of Our Perfect Person." You will share your group's perfect person with the entire class.

Activity 5.
Language

Challenge

Language: the expression or communication of thoughts and feelings by means of vocal sounds, and combinations of such sounds, to which meaning is attributed.

—Webster's New World Dictionary

In this activity, you will imagine how human beings first began using their voices for language. For example, an appropriate grunt brought the proper food to be passed around the fire. Another grunt might have expressed affection. A cry warned of danger.

Human beings also use nonverbal forms of communication. A smile expressed approval, a shrug says "I don't know," a snarl is a warning.

In Exercise #5, you will write down how you imagine language first began. Later, you will act out these scenes with others in the class.

Exercise #5

In the space below, write a scene describing how *vocal language* may have started. (Use your imagination and extra paper if needed.)

_____

_____

_____

Now, create a scene that shows how *written language* may have developed from spoken language.

_____

_____

_____

Look over the scenarios you just wrote. How difficult must life have been before language developed? You can think of yourself as a "language-enriched person." Write your answers to the following questions:

1. How has my ability to choose the right words helped my social life?

    _____

    _____

2. How has it helped me at school or work?

    _____

    _____

3. How has it helped me at home?

    _____

    _____

Putting It Together

In your small group, choose one scenario and act it out for the rest of the class.

When every group has had a chance to perform, get together into new groups and brainstorm ways you can learn new words that can help in your daily life.

Activity 6.
As I See It

Challenge

Three blind men were asked to describe an elephant. The first man walked up to the front of the elephant and felt its trunk.

"An elephant," he said, "is like a giant snake."

The second man walked up behind the elephant and felt its tail.

"An elephant," he said, "is like a rope."

The third man encountered the elephant's leg.

"You are both wrong," he said. "An elephant is like a tree trunk."

Which man was right?

In Exercise #6, you have a chance to experience blind guessing. You will guess what is inside a box, using only the eraser end of a pencil poked through some holes in the box to feel what is inside. The box is covered with a cloth so that no one can peek.

Exercise #6

Each group is to punch six to eight holes in the sides of a small box (such as a shoe box). Each member will secretly place a small object in the box. Each of the others then gets one minute to poke and prod inside the box with the eraser end of a pencil.

Say out loud what you observe. (For example, "It is soft and roundish.") You may not move or shake the box. Watch carefully, but do not talk. One member of the group should record the more important observations here:

Object   **Object**   **Object**

_____   _____   _____

_____   _____   _____

_____   _____   _____

Object   **Object**   **Object**

_____   _____   _____

_____   _____   _____

_____   _____   _____

Putting It Together

When each person has taken a turn poking around in the box and making observations, the group must pool all observations and then make educated guesses to come to *one* conclusion—a consensus.

Now exchange your still-concealed objects with other groups. Watch them observe and come to a consensus. Discuss the following questions in class:

▼ What process did the teams use to come to an agreement (if they did)?

▼ Who held out? Why and How?

▼ Who "visualized" what might be in the box?

▼ Who used more "logical," concrete clues?

▼ What strengths and weaknesses are there to each approach?

Activity 7.
Daydreaming

Challenge

Go with me on creative flights of daydreaming fantasy. You can go anywhere—see, hear, and experience anything you want. There are no limits!

Daydreaming is the creative flight necessary for planning future products or goals. Sometimes classroom daydreamers are frowned upon. You might be told you cannot leave the classroom—even in your mind.

As a student, I spent many hours in the principal's office because of daydreaming. Some teachers said I would never be successful in life because I was such a daydreamer. Now I write during and after entering the realm of daydreams—and I make a living at it!

In this exercise, you will jot down notes in response to some phrases. You will not be graded on spelling, grammar, or completeness. The idea is just to get your ideas on paper. You can even doodle or draw. Let your imagination run wild!

Exercise #7

Read each phrase and, in the space beside it, write down *anything* that comes into your mind. Don't worry about spelling or grammar or even complete sentences. Just write!

Cat on a fence _____

_____

Wild, white water river _____

_____

Tall, stately oak tree _____

_____

Student at a computer _homework_____

_____

Violent storm _____

_____

The perfect place to be _____

_____

Three carved figures on a table _____

_____

An unexplained bright light _aliens_____

_____

Putting It Together

Do you like to daydream? Do you see pictures? Hear? Feel? Smell? Do you keep your thoughts organized and "in control"? Or do you just let go? Do you have pleasant fantasies? Direct? Enjoy? Learn? Can you see the success in "just daydreaming"?

In your small group, use one or two of the following phrases to begin a story. Each member, in turn, will add a sentence to the story until the story finishes by itself.

▼ A huge sailing ship …

▼ A dying man …

▼ A deserted old house …

▼ A strange noise outside the window …

▼ An old chest in the attic …

▼ A hidden cave …

▼ A shadow in the woods …

Activity 8.
Motivation

Challenge

Motivation is the inner force that drives a person toward completion or satisfaction. Motivation must come from within; it cannot come from someone else. For example, you experience motivation when you see something you want and then put your energy into getting it.

What motivates you to succeed? What is the difference between motivation and incentive? In Exercise #8, you'll define different words that people sometimes confuse with motivation.

Exercise #8

People frequently misuse the following words when they describe "motivation." The words, however, have basically different meanings. Give a short definition of each word, an example in your life, and how each word differs from "motivation."

Motive _____

_____

Incentive _____

_____

Direct _____

_____

Regulate _____

_____

Compel _____

_____

Compulsion _____

Reward _____

_____

Control _____

_____

Overpower _____

_____

Spur _____

_____

Conduct _____

_____

Impulse_____

_____

Command _____

_____

Impel _____

_____

Putting It Together

In your small group, discuss the following questions together:

▼ What really gives me energy and gets me moving?

▼ When I'm feeling worn out, what revives my engine?

▼ Who or what stirs my soul?

▼ Who or what robs my energy?

Now discuss the ways you like to learn and to be taught. Share what you don't like about learning or being taught. Form a panel of "expert learners." Share your ideas about learning and teaching.

Activity 9.
The Describe-It Game

Challenge

If I tell you I'm thinking of something to eat, can you guess what it is? What if I tell you it's my favorite food? Or that it's a product of the sun? Can you guess now?

What if I say it's a yellow, sour fruit that grows on trees? And that it's used to make pies and a cool summer drink? Did you guess it's a lemon?

The words we use to describe things (or ourselves) can be abstract or concrete, general or specific. But each leaves a definite impression in the minds of others.

In Exercise #9, you'll play a game called *Describe It*, in which you'll move from abstract, vague descriptions to concrete, specific ones.

Exercise #9

To play this game, a player attempts to describe a word by giving examples and descriptions (such as synonyms and antonyms). The class must guess the player's word.

Round 1

Each person gets two minutes to describe a word—someone watching the time should say when 30 seconds are left. Start out by describing the word in very general terms, but as you continue, become more precise until the word can be guessed in the last 30 seconds. No guesses are made until 90 seconds have elapsed. The best description cannot be guessed until the last 30 seconds. Each person has a turn to present a word.

Words You May Use   **How to Describe the Word**

_____   _____

_____   _____

_____   _____
_____   _____
_____   _____
_____   _____

Round 2

Try to give one- or two-sentence descriptions so clearly that the word is guessed immediately.

Words You Will Use   **Your Simple Description**

_____   _____
_____   _____
_____   _____
_____   _____
_____   _____

Putting It Together

In your small groups, take turns answering these questions:

▼ Do I like to use words to express myself?

▼ Where am I really good at it?

▼ Where do I need improvement?

▼ Why should I improve?

▼ Is it true that the more clearly I express myself, the more successful I appear to others? Why?

What were your reactions to this game? Work together with your group to improve it, making the rules clearer and easier to follow. Share your revised game with the total group.

Activity 10.
A Place for Everything

Challenge

It takes practice to improve communication with others. We are not born with communication as a gift. We develop it as a skill.

Practice communication by giving and receiving instructions and learn by watching others struggle.

It's easy to watch someone else mess up and to think, "I can do that better!" But the only way to really learn to do something well is to practice it. In Exercise #10, you'll practice sending clear, understandable messages. You'll also have the chance to practice active listening.

Exercise #10

Each team should have a set of the following designs:

▼ 2 large squares of paper (4" x 4")

▼ 2 small circles (2" in diameter)

▼ 4 small squares (2" x 2")

▼ 4 small rectangles (2" x 3")

▼ 4 small triangles (2" base)

▼ 2 large circles (4" in diameter)

▼ 2 large rectangles (4" x 6")

Two persons sit back-to-back. On the desk in front of each is an identical set of shapes. One player is a Sender; the other a silent Receiver. The Sender's task is to use the materials to make a design, describing clearly what he or she is making, so that the Receiver can duplicate it (without looking at the Sender's pattern). Continue this until everyone has a chance to send and receive. Observers can answer the following questions:

What are the most common mistakes in sending?

_____

_____

_____

_____

List what makes a good sender.

_____

_____

_____

_____

List what makes a good receiver.

_____

_____

_____

_____

Putting It Together

In your group, describe your participation as a receiver and/or sender (how involved and interested you were, not how good you were). Take turns answering these questions:

▼ What did I observe about my own sending and receiving?

▼ What did I learn about my ability to communicate clearly?

▼ What can I do to improve my communications skills?

Activity 11.
There's Only One You

⌐ Challenge ──────────────────

Your uniqueness implies some kinds of differences when compared to "the average." Where do you fit?

In Exercise #11, you'll complete sentences with spontaneous responses. Your responses will be different from everyone else's. No two people think or respond in exactly the same way. Those differences in the way we think, behave, and respond is what enables us to continue to learn, grow, and evolve as a society.

Exercise #11

"I statements" are good ways to measure your uniqueness. Finish each sentence below with your own concerns in mind:

I am _____

_____

I wish _____

_____

I like _____

_____

I frequently _____

_____

I was _____

_____

I should _____

_____

I will _____

_____

I want _____

_____

I have _____

_____

I suspect _____

_____

I will be _____

_____

I can _____

_____

I would like to be_____

_____

I rarely_____

_____

I know_____

_____

 # Putting It Together

Go back over your responses and check three that you really like about yourself.

In your group, share your responses on each incomplete sentence. Are any of your responses similar to another member's? Talk about your similarities and your differences.

▼ How many of your responses were unique?

▼ How many were shared by others?

Activity 12.
Think-Tank Products

Challenge

A think tank is a small group in which members share thoughts and feelings about a specific task or problem and then proceed to develop a "product." The product can be further research, a visual or audio display, a report, a newsletter, and so on. In short, the product can be experienced by others.

In Exercise #12, you'll use the basic group processes described below to design an "ideal" learning situation:

▼ **Open Discussions** can be held in small or large groups and usually are led by a facilitator.

▼ **The Circle** involves face-to-face communication in a group seated in (surprise!) a circle. The opportunity to talk is passed from person to person around the circle.

▼ **Panels** usually involve presentations of opinions by a group from the front of the room.

▼ A **Colloquium** is a team that represents the audience and interviews or asks questions of resource people.

▼ In a **Forum**, opposing points of view are presented. This is followed by questions and answers from the audience.

▼ In a **Symposium**, a few students present their work, then answer questions from the floor.

▼ In **Role-Playing**, individuals or small groups act out a situation. This method can be used to find alternative solutions to problems or to get a definite point across to the audience.

In the exercise, you will also use *brainstorming* and *ranking*. Brainstorming is a process in which everyone calls out ideas, whatever comes to mind, and *all* ideas are jotted down, without criticism of them. There are a few important rules in brainstorming:

▼ No criticism is allowed. Every idea is potentially great!

▼ The key is to generate *lots* of ideas. Initially, the goal is quantity, not quality.

▼ Wacky is okay; just let the ideas fly.

▼ It's okay to add to the ideas of others. Coattailing is great!

Ranking is the process of assigning levels of importance, then listing the responses in that order. (So, for example, you write 1, 2, 3, etc., next to each statement, then list the statements in the order you ranked them.)

Exercise #12

Use the think-tank process to design an "ideal" learning situation. The process of developing a product within your think tank can be as follows:

1. Brainstorm in a group.

2. List your ideas in order of importance (ranking).

3. Assume responsibilities (as opposed to assigning them).

4. Let others know how the product is developing.

5. Refine the rough product.

6. Give the presentation/product.

7. Evaluate as a group or individually and provide feedback (such as satisfaction, celebration, awards, certificates).

Use the following chart to log your progress. (Approximately 20 minutes.)

Check When Completed	The Process	Time Limit (Minutes)	Notes and Suggestions
❏	1. Brainstorm ideas	3	_____
❏	2. Make choice	3	_____
❏	3. Determine course of action	3	_____
❏	4. Refine idea	3	_____
❏	5. Present idea	3	_____
❏	6. Evaluate idea's success	3	_____

Putting It Together

In your small group, use the think-tank process to make a product of your choice. Use the same process and time limits. When you've completed the process, discuss whether the process went more smoothly the second time. Discuss any rough spots and ideas to smooth them out. Share your *product* and *process* with the total group

Activity 13.
Make a "Somethink"

Challenge

A "somethink" is unique!

Are you confused? Good! Now do Exercise #13.

Exercise #13

Get into groups of four people. Place *one* sheet of paper between you. Your task is to make a "somethink." You have no other instructions. Go!

Watching everyone make a "somethink," decide how each member contributed to the group. Write the name in the box that describes the efforts of each person.

Fill in your own opinions of how each member did in the chart below. Then compare your opinions with the opinions of the other members of your group.

	Group 1	Group 2	Group 3	Group 4
Good organizer	Jon			
Pleasant, helpful	Jon			
Blocked group efforts	Heather			
Too humorous				
Too quiet				
Talked too much	Doug			
Blocked progress	Doug			

Putting It Together

In your small group, take turns answering the following questions:

▼ How do I feel about such unclear instructions?

I like it, it's easier than having specific instructions

▼ How did I do?

good

▼ Who took charge?

Heather & me

▼ Did we do okay?

yes

▼ How could I do better?

we couldn't

▼ How can I tell others how to improve?

▼ How can I best compliment?

▼ How did each person contribute to the project?

everyone helped

▼ What was our group's biggest problem?

▼ Discuss your differences and similarities.

Activity 14.
How I See You

Challenge

"Everybody likes me!"

The key word in this activity is respect. In Exercise #14, you'll find out what other people really think of you. And you'll have the opportunity to tell others honestly and caringly what you think of them. Be honest, sincere, and respectful.

Exercise #14

Take this page to several people in the classroom who like you. Ask each person to write a short phrase saying something nice that the individual really feels about you. Ask each person to be sincere. Avoid mixed messages, and do not talk during the experience.

1. _____

   _____

   _____

2. _____

   _____

   _____

3. _____

   _____

   _____

4. _____

   _____

   _____

5. _____

_____

_____

6. _____

_____

_____

_____

7. _____

_____

_____

8. _____

_____

_____

Putting It Together

In your small group, discuss the following questions:

▼ How am I after this experience?

▼ These are three feelings I have after this exercise:

▼ These are three thoughts I have about this exercise:

▼ Here are three "new" things I saw about myself:

▼ Here are three ways I am different:

Activity 15.

Levels of Importance

Challenge

Some things are more important to you than they are to others. That's the way it should be. Imagine how it would be if everything had equal importance in your life.

What is really important to you?

In this exercise, there are no "right" and "wrong" answers—only what you think and feel. Be honest in your responses, and be courteous and respectful of others' responses.

Exercise #15

List 5 things that are very important to you. Write them on the lines below:

_____

_____

_____

_____

_____

Now decide which is *the* most important thing. Put a "1" in front of it. Put a "2" in front of the next most important thing. Do this down to the least important ("5").

List six classes you take in school. Assign levels of importance to these classes.

1. _____

2. _____

3. _____

4. _____

5. _____

6. _____

Why is "1" so important?

_____

_____

_____

_____

Why is "6" not as important?

_____

_____

_____

List five of your activities outside school. Assign levels of importance to these activities.

1. _____

2. _____

3. _____

4. _____

5. _____

Think of five people you know; then list your feelings toward each of them, along with why you feel this way, and assign levels of importance to these feelings.

1. _____

2. _____

3. _____

4. _____

5. _____

Putting It Together

Share your important things, classes, activities, responsibilities, and feelings with other members of your small group. How do others' ideas compare with yours? What conflicts do the differences cause? How can you resolve these conflicts?

Discuss issues that don't get solved easily, such as religious or political ideas. Can you hold different religious views and still be friends with someone? What about different values? List possible solutions to conflicts caused by these differences. Thank one another for sharing such important matters.

Activity 16.

Successfully Unique

Challenge

"The Creator" (however you envision that) made you and threw away the mold!

In what way is that statement true? How does your uniqueness affect the way you communicate? How does what you meant to say get misinterpreted and perhaps cause misunderstandings and conflict? How does "uniqueness" contribute to communication gaps? What is uniqueness, anyway?

You may like to think you communicate clearly. But the reality is that when you say something, several messages are being sent: (1) what you mean to say, (2) what comes out of your mouth, (3) what goes in the other person's ears, and (4) what that person thinks he or she heard.

In Exercise #16, you'll look up definitions of the terms *unique* and *success*. What does the dictionary say they mean? What do they mean to you? These may be similar, or they may be very different.

Exercise #16

For this exercise, you will need several different dictionaries. You will look up the definitions of two words—*unique* and *successful*—in each dictionary and choose the definition you like best for each. How do the definitions differ? How are they the same? Why did you choose the one you liked best?

Write a dictionary definition of "unique." (Use different dictionaries to find the meaning you like best.)

_____

_____

Why do you like this definition?

_____

_____

Rewrite the dictionary definition in your own words.

_____

_____

Now, look up the term "successful."

_____

_____

Write a dictionary definition you like.

_____

_____

Define "successful" in your own words.

_____

_____

Putting It Together

What does it mean "to be successful"? Who is successful? How did they get that way. Were they born with success? Did they learn it? How did they develop and nourish their success? In your small groups, discuss how you define success—what it means and how you recognize it. Answer the following questions:

▼ Make a group list of people who are successful. How do you measure their success?

▼ Now think of a person you know who is successful. Tell the group what about that person makes him or her successful.

▼ Which qualities of that person do you think are inborn, and which are learned (acquired)?

▼ Now list three of your own qualities that are inborn and three that are acquired.

▼ In what ways do you feel successful right now?

Do your best to communicate your inborn and acquired qualities to others in your group. Be aware that the message may not be heard and understood as you intended. Listen closely as other members attempt to communicate clearly.

Activity 17.
A Successful Person

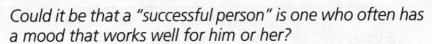

Challenge

Success is an attitude that works well. An attitude is a state of mind or a mood.

Could it be that a "successful person" is one who often has a mood that works well for him or her?

In this exercise, you will determine the qualities that make up a successful person. What mood exemplifies the successful person? What is it that he or she does that exudes success? How can *you* develop a successful mood? Is it an immediate or a long-term thing? Or is it both?

Exercise #17

In the space below, write down the first name only of a person you think of as successful.

_____

List three specific "successful" things that person does. For example, perhaps he runs an outboard repair shop well enough to make a living and do the things he wants to do in life.

1. _____

2. _____

3. _____

Write what you think that person's overall mood or attitude is.

_____

_____

_____

Rewrite your dictionary definition of "successful" from Exercise #16 in the space below.

_____

_____

Does the person you listed above seem to fit the definition?

_____

_____

In what ways does he or she match the definition?

_____

_____

In what ways is he or she different?

_____

_____

 # Putting It Together

In your small group, take turns answering the following questions:

▼ Why did I list the person I did?

▼ What do I like about that person's success?

▼ What does that tell me about myself?

▼ How am I like that person?

▼ How am I different?

Let others in your group help you define ways you are like and not like your successful person.

Discuss things that successful people *do*, giving concrete examples.

Activity 18.

Ways I Am Already Successful

Challenge

Say the following phrases to yourself.

I am beginning to sense that success is not something that I achieve (after much hard work, at some future day).

I am now sure that "being successful" is simply accepting the progress I have already made and who I already am at this moment.

I now assume the attitude of being successful.

In this exercise, you will have a chance to look at your own successes. What are you good at? What can you do? Do you have a natural talent? Do you have skills you've worked hard to acquire? What makes you unique? What makes you a success?

Exercise #18

In the space below, list three things you have *learned to do* well (with your hands, brain, body):

1. _____

2. _____

3. _____

Now list two talents you have (things that seem to come easily to you):

1. _____

2. _____

List below three ways *you are* that make you a special person.

1. _____

2. _____

3. _____

List three qualities you already have as a friend:

1. _____

2. _____

3. _____

Use the answers to the statements above to check the appropriate boxes in the chart below.

	Low	Medium	High
Skills			
Personality			
Friendship			

Putting It Together

Share with your group some ways your life is already successful. Take turns answering the following questions:

▼ What am I proud of in my life?

▼ What comes easily to me?

▼ What have I learned to do that was hard, but I did it anyway?

Practice an attitude of success—let it show in the way you walk and talk, in your tone of voice and the way you dress, in the company you keep and the activities you participate in.

Each group member should say out loud, one at a time:

> I am already successful
> in what I *do* (my skills),
> in who I *am* (my personality),
> and in my qualities as a friend.

Activity 19.

Seeds of Service 1

Challenge

You can have one of two attitudes:

1. Get what you can.

2. Give what you are able.

Instead of thinking of ways to make money, I will create ways to give—to be of service to others.

In this exercise, the focus is on *service*, not on *reward*. How can you give of yourself to help others? What time, talents, and skills do you have that you can use? Of course, there's no such thing as complete selflessness, because whenever you give of yourself, you *do* receive a reward—knowing you are serving others is a reward in itself.

Exercise #19

In this exercise, you will use the brainstorming technique to come up with ideas about how you can serve others by giving of yourself. Can you volunteer at a local community agency? Can you help a younger child learn something new? Can you help out at home? Write your ideas down just as fast as they come to you, even if some don't look practical. Don't try to evaluate or critique your ideas.

_____

_____

_____

_____

_____

_____

Putting It Together

In your group, go through your list of ideas with others. Maybe they can suggest ways of implementing some of your ideas. Maybe they have new ideas you hadn't thought of. Discuss the following questions:

▼ What is the "pay-off" of helping others?

▼ Name a satisfying experience you had helping others.

▼ Is it easier for you to give help or to receive help?

▼ How can you help someone who doesn't seem to want your help but really needs it?

Activity 20.

Planning and Scheduling

Challenge

You have valuable gifts to give: your time and your energy. Planning how you will use these gifts lets you use them wisely.

You can spend lots of time using little energy (like sitting in a boring lecture). Or you can expend lots of energy in a short time (as in sports or an intense game). How you spend your time and energy is up to you. *You* are the only one who can decide what you will do with your time and your life.

In Exercise # 20, you'll do some brainstorming of ways you could spend your energy. Remember, in brainstorming you should jot down the ideas (no matter how ridiculous they seem) just as fast as they come to you. Evaluating the ideas comes later. For now, just get them on paper.

Exercise #20

Use the personal brainstorming technique to list all the ways you expend energy. Record your thoughts as fast as they enter your mind. Don't try to evaluate or critique what you write.

_____

_____

_____

Now write down specific places or ways you expend only a little bit of energy:

_____

_____

_____

_____

Putting It Together

In your small group, discuss the following questions:

▼ Who wants more of my time and energy than I want to give?

▼ What do they want of me? Why?

▼ Is it the way they go about it or what they want that bothers me?

▼ How can I help them ask me differently?

▼ How can I let them know they expect the wrong things?

▼ What do I expect from others in my life?

▼ Am I realistic?

▼ Do I allow others to make mistakes?

▼ How can I change my expectations?

▼ Am I open to change?

Now discuss with group members your plans for avoiding conflicts with others who demand your time and energy.

Activity 21.
Needs

Challenge

A need is a necessity, something that's required. Alternatively, a need can be a lack of something you want.

What is the difference between a *need* and a *want*? Think about basic human needs, like food, air, and water. What are some other basic needs? Are mine different from yours? Or do we all have the same basic needs?

Look up the definitions of the following words in a dictionary:

▼ Need _____   Want _____

▼ Desire _____   Requirement _____

▼ Necessity _____   Lack _____

Is love a need or a desire? Is respect a necessity or a want? Is acceptance a need? What about freedom?

In Exercise #21, you'll have a chance to think about and rank your needs.

Exercise #21

Some needs are obvious. Human beings need clean air, water, and food. Other needs are less tangible. In the chart below are three things many people define as needs. Think about your need for each; then circle whether your need is low, medium, or high. Finally, jot down an idea or two on how you can best meet this need.

Need	My Level of Need	How Can I Best Meet This Need?
Acceptance	Low Medium High	
Self-worth	Low Medium High	
Freedom to explore	Low Medium High	

In the space below, list some other needs you have. Circle your level of need, and jot down ideas of how you can meet the need.

Need	My Level of Need	How Can I Best Meet This Need?
	Low Medium High	
	Low Medium High	
	Low Medium High	
	Low Medium High	
	Low Medium High	

Putting It Together

In your small group, discuss the following questions:

▼ How are the needs of others the same or different from my own?

▼ What words will I use to describe the needs of others?

▼ What happens when my needs conflict with your needs?

▼ How can we resolve our conflicting needs?

As a group, list some ways that your needs differ from those of one another.

Now list some needs you all have in common.

Finally, work together to define the following terms—ending with definitions you all agree upon:

▼ Necessity   ▼ Want

▼ Desire   ▼ Lack

Take turns giving examples of each term from your own life. What is a necessity for you? What do you lack? Desire? Want? Need?

Activity 22.
Feelings Defined

Challenge

I'm ecstatic. I'm so happy and content that I don't want to hold it back. I feel a nice flow of joy all through me.

What makes you "ecstatic"? What makes you smile? Who or what can brighten your day? Our feelings have a profound influence on our lives. But do they control us, or do we control them?

Can you develop an attitude of success? Can you cultivate happiness? First, you have to define what happiness means to you. Complete Exercise #22 to find out what makes you happy.

Exercise #22

Write four words that describe the good feelings you have when you are "happy." Describe those feelings in as much detail as possible. Do you feel warm? Giggly? Secure? Use a dictionary and thesaurus to find a definition of each feeling. Then write your own definition, in your own words. Write down an example of when you've experienced these feelings in your life.

Feeling 1: _____

Dictionary Definition: _____

_____

_____

My Own Definition: _____

_____

_____

When Have I Felt This Way? _____

_____

_____

Feeling 2: _____

    Dictionary Definition: _____

    _____

    _____

    My Own Definition: _____

    _____

    _____

    When Have I Felt This Way? _____

    _____

    _____

Feeling 3: _____

    Dictionary Definition: _____

    _____

    _____

    My Own Definition: _____

    _____

    _____

    When Have I Felt This Way? _____

    _____

    _____

Feeling 4: _____

    Dictionary Definition: _____

    _____

    _____

My Own Definition: _____

_____

_____

When Have I Felt This Way? _____

_____

_____

Putting It Together

In your small group, discuss the following questions:

▼ Name a person who seems happy. How does that person behave?

▼ How does he or she handle disappointments?

▼ What does a good day *feel* like?

▼ What makes a good day?

▼ Can you make a good day happen? How?

Activity 23.

Discarded Computer Parts

Challenge

According to Roget's Thesaurus, *the word "useless" can mean any number of things, including rubbish, trashy, junky, rubble, scrap, waste, chaff, jetsam, litter, fruitless, inept, unproductive, and unfunctional.*

What some see as useless might be experienced by others as useful.

Do you ever feel "useless"? What makes you feel like a failure? Making mistakes? Being wrong? Not fitting in? When you are feeling "useless," there are good news and bad news to remember. That bad news is, nobody's perfect. The good news is … nobody's perfect.

Learning to accept our mistakes and failures with a sense of humor, and deciding to learn from them, can go a long way toward turning those failures into successes.

In Exercise #23, you'll think about "recycling" your failures into successes.

Exercise #23

For this exercise, you'll engage in a bit of make-believe. Pretend you are an electronic computer component that has been tossed into the trash. Now answer the following questions:

What part are you?

_____

Why were you discarded?

_____

Who put you here?

_____

Should you be recycled? Why?

_____

In the space below, describe a recycling process that will make you a valuable part again.

_____

_____

_____

Putting It Together

Discuss with your group the feeling of not fitting in. Complete the following sentences to get started:

▼ The time I most remember not fitting in was

▼ The people who were there at the time were

▼ The reason I didn't "fit" was

▼ I felt

Now, within the group, brainstorm ways in which you could have handled the situation differently. What could you have done to change the situation? Or how could you have accepted it better?

Activity 24.
My Problem

Challenge

I accept that I am human, and I can fall short.

I also realize that I can grow and change.

Finding solutions to problems takes thoughtful consideration. Sometimes, when we're in the middle of a problem, it's helpful to stop, take a step back, and look at the causes of the problem. Then perhaps we will see the solution.

But, you might ask, what if there is no solution? Then perhaps the answer is to change the way we react to the problem. Remember, we cannot always control life. *But we can always decide how we will respond.*

In Exercise #24, you'll list problems other people might have, and then list possible solutions to those problems. Learning to look at someone else's problems objectively is good practice for dealing with your own.

Exercise #24

In the space below, list four problems that other people have. They can be problems someone you know is having, or problems you have read about. Under each problem, write four possible causes of the problem.

For example,

Problem: I'm almost always late for work.

Causes: I don't get up early enough.

I take too long finding an outfit to wear.

I don't allow enough time for the commute.

Every morning when I let the dog out, he jumps the fence, and I have to chase him down.

Problem: _____

Causes: _____

_____

_____

Problem: _____

Causes _____

_____

_____

_____

Problem: _____

Causes: _____

_____

_____

Problem: _____

Causes: _____

_____

_____

Putting It Together

What problems do you have in your life? How do they affect your life? What are some possible causes? How can you handle them more effectively?

In your small group, talk about problems people have, possible causes, and inappropriate and successful approaches to solving them.

Now it's time for a role-play. Decide as a group on a specific "life" problem. Who is involved in the problem? What role does each person involved play? Now assign those roles to members of the group. Within character, discuss the problem and possible solutions. Share your findings with the total group.

Activity 25.

Contracting

Challenge

Contract with yourself for success!

A contract is an agreement between two or more persons *to do* something or *to be* a certain way. You can contract to perform a service or to produce a product. This is done in an agreed upon way for a specified reward or compensation.

In Exercise #25, you will find a list of activities you can "contract" with your teacher to do for extra credit or for exemption from one homework assignment or for whatever other "payment" the two of you decide upon. The point is this: Once you sign the contract, you are bound by the contract. *You must do what you say you will do.*

Exercise #25

In this exercise, you will be contracting to do a task(s) for an agreed upon reward (a grade, extra credit, homework credits, etc.). You and your teacher will sign and date the contract when you both agree on the tasks and rewards.

Teacher's Initials	Possible Tasks	Compensation
	Research 10 words that relate to being successful.	
	Make a test of "Being Successful," matching 20 words in the left column with definitions or examples in the right column.	
	Write two, single-page biographies of successful people.	
	Draw and explain a famous invention.	
	Write a five-minute script about a successful attitude.	

Teacher's Initials	Possible Tasks	Compensation
	Write a two-page account of your typical successful day, from start to finish.	
	Arrange for a successful person to speak to your class.	
	Create a puppet show, play, or skit describing success.	
	Make a complete bibliography of success-related materials.	
	Make and teach a 10-minute teaching unit on the topic of success, with pre- and post-tests.	
	Make a five-minute audiovisual presentation on poor attitudes.	
	Other project(s) of your choice:	

Dated

_____

Signed

Contractor _____

Instructor/Facilitator _____

Putting It Together

In your small group, discuss the following questions:

▼ Have I done my best to decide on a task and contract for the reward?

▼ What have I learned about how I "sell" myself and how I "push" for a fair compensation?

▼ Do I feel more pressure to complete the project I have contracted to do?

▼ Why or why not?

Activity 26.
Buried Talents

Challenge

An employer gave two employees $2,000 each with the instruction to "use it wisely until I return." One employee provided a service to people and realized a fair profit. The other fearfully buried the money until the boss returned. Which employee used the money wisely?

How can you make money by uncovering your buried talents? What are buried talents, anyway? A buried talent is something, anything, you do well. Maybe you sing or play a musical instrument. Perhaps you do math or read very well. Are you physically strong? Do you have a knack for growing things? Can you draw, run, or get along well with almost anyone? All of these (and countless other things) are talents. And you can use your talents to help others *and* to make a profit. In Exercise 26, you'll get a chance to try it out.

Exercise #26

Your task is to take $10 and turn it into $50 in three months or less by providing a service or a product to the world (those around you, your classmates, your family, or your neighbors). Your dollars will grow when you receive a fair profit for the energy you expend in your service or product.

For a product, you can use your $10 to buy materials you need to make something (for example, paper and materials for a newsletter); you may buy something and sell it for a profit; or you may buy and gradually "trade up," and then sell.

A service can be almost anything. Can you give your friends haircuts? Mow your neighbor's lawn? Run errands for your parents? Wash cars? Draw portraits? For a service, use the "personal brainstorming" exercise that follows.

Below are 10 ways I can increase my service to the world.

1. _____

2. _____

3. _____

4. _____

5. _____

6. _____

7. _____

8. _____

9. _____

10. _____

Rank the three best ideas.

First: _____

Second: _____

Third: _____

Use your first choice to write a plan to begin as soon as possible.

_____

_____

_____

_____

_____

_____

Use separate sheets of paper to list alternative plans for your second and third ideas.

Keep exact records (to the penny). Do not spend—invest! After you earn $50, give yourself a percentage of the profit. Reinvest the rest. Write "Service to the World" on your books, posters, bumper-stickers—think *service*, not profit! Report your plans, progress, and profits to your instructor. Providing a service to the world automatically brings a reward. The "payoff" may just be personal satisfaction rather than financial rewards.

Putting It Together

In your small group, discuss the following questions:

▼ Do I really believe that I "get" when I "give"?

▼ How do I feel about being of service to the world?

▼ Is it more important to serve, or to make money?

▼ Can I do both at once?

Remember, there are no right or wrong answers. For example, if you're on the verge of homelessness, it's more than important to make money—it's a necessity.

Activity 27.
Intelligence

┌─ **Challenge** ──────────────

We should take care not to make intellect our god; it has, of course, powerful muscles, but no personality.

—Albert Einstein

What is "intelligence"? Is it knowing a lot of information? Is it creativity? Is it being able to figure things out? Can you be intelligent in one area, and not in another? Is there a difference between education and intelligence? In this exercise, you'll explore these questions and look at your own intelligence, creativity, and talents.

Exercise #27

Look up the definition of *intelligence* in a dictionary. Write that definition below:

_____

In the space below, write your own definition of intelligence:

_____

_____

List three ways intelligence can be tested.

1. _____

2. _____

3. _____

Now look up the definition of creativity and write it in the space below:

_____

_____

How does creativity differ from intelligence? Write your answer below:

_____

_____

_____

List five ways you have been creative. Remember, *creative* does not always mean *artistic*.

1. _____

2. _____

3. _____

4. _____

5. _____

In the space below, list three "creations" of yours:

1. _____

2. _____

3. _____

Putting It Together

With your small group, discuss the following questions:

▼ Is being creative different from being inventive?

▼ What about being productive?

▼ Can you *learn* to be more creative, or is it just something you're born with?

As a group, make a list of ways you have already demonstrated your "smarts" in this class.

I AM ALREADY SUCCESSFUL

Activity 28.
It's Your Choice

Challenge _____

I shall be telling this with a sigh
Somewhere ages and ages hence:
Two roads diverged in a wood, and I—
I took the one less traveled by,
And that has made all the difference.

—*Robert Frost*

How much choice do you have in life? In school? Do you decide what classes you will take? Do you decide how much time you will study? Do you decide how well you will do? What about after school? Who will decide what work you will do with your life? Remember this: Your career choices are *yours*—either by your own decisions or by leaving the choice to someone else.

Exercise #28

Read each statement; then circle if you agree or disagree with it. On the lines below each statement, explain why you agree or disagree.

Many people are concerned about my best interests.   Agree   Disagree

_____

_____

_____

People with special skills are more likely to be employed.   Agree   Disagree

_____

_____

_____

64 ▷ I AM *ALREADY* SUCCESSFUL

The people helping me choose my course of study know what is best for me.
Agree   Disagree

_____

_____

_____

The more I put into my education, the better education I get.   Agree   Disagree

_____

_____

_____

The more years of schooling I have, the more successful I will be in life.
Agree   Disagree

_____

_____

_____

 # Putting It Together

In your small group, discuss the following questions:

▼ If I could do anything I wanted for my career, I would …

▼ What would I have to do to achieve that goal?

▼ Who will decide my career?

Activity 29.
Do You Agree?

Challenge

Opinions are made to be changed—or how is the truth to be got at?

—Lord Byron

Everyone has an opinion about what is right and wrong. This is your chance to offer some of your own opinions.

Exercise #29

Read each statement. Decide if you agree or disagree with each one; then circle the appropriate response. Put an *X* beside the ones you *strongly agree* or *strongly disagree* with.

You should always show trust and confidence.	Agree	Disagree
If you are right, you don't have to see the other person's side.	Agree	Disagree
You should always be fair and just.	Agree	Disagree
It's okay to compare one person with another.	Agree	Disagree
People change faster for friends than for family.	Agree	Disagree
Keep rules simple and few.	Agree	Disagree
Keep problems to yourself. Don't let outsiders in.	Agree	Disagree
Be kind and courteous.	Agree	Disagree
There is no "democracy"—someone is always in charge.	Agree	Disagree
The whole family should suffer if someone is angry or down.	Agree	Disagree
You should satisfy your own needs first.	Agree	Disagree
Don't plan anything so you won't be disappointed.	Agree	Disagree

Never say harsh or unkind words.	Agree	Disagree
Never show anger or dislike.	Agree	Disagree
My goal is to be perfect.	Agree	Disagree

Putting It Together

Read each statement in your small group and discuss it. Try to get 100 percent agreement on one of them. Can you do it? Discuss why you can't always get complete agreement.

Activity 30.
Test Me

Challenge

"I am more than the results of my tests."

Test results can be helpful. In the lower grades, test results help teachers place you in suitable classes. Test results also help your teachers monitor your progress in different subjects. More importantly, test results can help *you* make *your own choices* of classes and training courses.

Exercise #30

Get the results of two tests you have taken in the last year—one academic and one personal interest test. Describe what you learned about yourself from these tests.

Test 1 (Academic)

Results:

_____

_____

What you learned about yourself:

_____

_____

_____

How this helps your career choice:

_____

_____

_____

Test 2 (Interest)

Results:

_____

_____

What you learned about yourself:

_____

_____

_____

How this helps your career choice:

_____

_____

_____

Putting It Together

In your small group, answer these questions:

▼ What have you learned about yourself from tests?

▼ Do tests really tell you whether you are successful?

▼ How can you use test results?

Share ways to get information from your school files that you can use to your benefit (for example, on job applications and school applications).

Simulation 1:
The Game

You have completed the activities of Section 1. Now put what you have learned about yourself to work in *The Game*:

A major game company has asked your small group to develop a challenging, high-quality language game that can relax and amuse young adults as it teaches them to communicate easily and with satisfaction.

The company has set some guidelines for you to follow. The game must be:

▼ Stimulating and enjoyable

▼ Organized, with clear directions

▼ Of marketable quality

▼ Instructive, but not "stuffy"

▼ Noncompetitive—everyone wins, nobody loses

Begin by brainstorming what your game should be.

_____

_____

_____

_____

Present your first rough ideas for the game to your team. When you have come to an agreement about the product, as a group, develop your characters, game board design (or computer screen), directions, manipulation devices, color scheme, and so on.

_____

_____

_____

_____

Now present your game plan to the entire class. Let other groups critique your game; then incorporate their ideas to make your game even better.

_____

_____

_____

Finally, make your game. And play it!

Evaluation of *The Game*

After you have played your game for the first time, complete the following evaluation form.

Exercise

Characteristic	Low				High
Stimulating and enjoyable	1	2	3	4	5
Incentive for finishing	1	2	3	4	5
Instructional	1	2	3	4	5
Organized	1	2	3	4	5
Targeted age and group	1	2	3	4	5
Marketable product	1	2	3	4	5
Originality	1	2	3	4	5
Other	1	2	3	4	5
	1	2	3	4	5
	1	2	3	4	5
	1	2	3	4	5

List problems with and solutions for the first draft of the game:

_____

_____

_____

_____

_____

Revise and evaluate your game as many times as needed. Have others play and evaluate your game.

Small Group Inventory 1

Now that you have completed the first simulation in this book, take a few minutes to write down your opinions of the small group you have been working with. Think carefully about how your group worked together. (Complete the form individually.)

Characteristic	Low	Average	High
1. Level of sincerity			
You all tried to do your best	1	2	3
You all attempted to learn more	1	2	3
Comments			
2. Research			
Used many sources	1	2	3
Clear, straightforward sharing of material	1	2	3
Comments			

Characteristic	Low	Average	High
3. Awareness			
You attempted to listen to the ideas of others	1	2	3
Level at which the group communicates ideas	1	2	3
Comments			
4. Cooperation			
Level at which you worked together	1	2	3
You tried to understand the needs of others	1	2	3
Comments			
5. Product			
You completed your work	1	2	3
Clarity of work	1	2	3
Appearance of work	1	2	3
Comments			
6. Your Overall Satisfaction with the Group			
Comments			

Self-Inventory 1

Now evaluate yourself. How are you doing so far? Before you begin answering these questions, review your responses in Section 1 and what you have learned about yourself.

Ask yourself these questions honestly and with a fair degree of self-examination.

Characteristic	Low	Average	High
1. My Level of Sincerity			
I desired to do my best	1	2	3
I attempted to learn more	1	2	3
I tried to cooperate	1	2	3
2. My Research			
I used many sources	1	2	3
I wrote clear, straightforward responses in book	1	2	3
I tried to find more resources	1	2	3
3. My Awareness of Myself			
I discovered new things	1	2	3
I tried to improve	1	2	3
I worked on personal challenges	1	2	3
4. My Awareness of Others			
I cooperated in my group	1	2	3
Level of my ability to communicate ideas	1	2	3
My ability to assist others	1	2	3
5. My Written and Oral Product			
Quality of my oral report	1	2	3
Excellence of my written work	1	2	3
Amount of preparation for oral or written work	1	2	3

Characteristic	Low	Average	High
6. Carryover Outside School			
Homework	1	2	3
Degree of interest in my studies	1	2	3
Hobbies and interests that relate to this course	1	2	3
7. My Overall Sense of Personal Satisfaction			
My satisfaction with my personal growth	1	2	3
My ability to be a friend	1	2	3
My awareness of the world	1	2	3
Amount of available energy I used	1	2	3
Degree I progressed compared to my potential	1	2	3

Moving On

After completing the first section of this book, you should know more about yourself than you did at the start.

You should begin to see that you are *already* a success. This first section of the book and its game simulation have shown you your own "uniqueness."

In Section 2, you will see how successful you already are with those around you. You may be surprised to find out that the members of your small group already see you as successful. As you experience the next section, you will find your success as seen through the eyes of others.

Don't forget, there are no "right" or "wrong" answers here, only differences of opinion!

2
SECTION

Success with Others

"Being successful" means being able to share your ideas and feelings with others. The people you work with in this class understand themselves as unique, and as you do these exercises together, your classmates will learn to understand why you are unique. As you express yourselves, you will discover your similarities.

The key to being successful is realizing *you are already a successful person.* You are successful not because of who you are or what you accomplish, but because you are planning, trying, doing, and being. Success is not far away in the future. Success is an attitude you can learn and start to practice right now.

In Section 1, you focused on discovering your own unique self. You explored what is important in your life, revealed your feelings, and studied your ability to learn. In short, you saw yourself as unique.

In Section 2, you will focus on the people around you. Working with your group, you will interview others, discuss, evaluate, and make decisions. You will share feelings and reactions, first in small groups and then in your large group.

You will begin this section by learning how to conduct an interview. You will study your classmates' interests and attitudes, rather than your own. This is the first step in learning to work successfully with others. Many of the activities that follow ask you to consider what the other people in your group think and feel.

In this section, you will work together toward the simulation *The Business*, which draws on the full knowledge and creativity of the game team you put together for your first simulation.

Activity 31.
Interviewing Techniques

Challenge

Questions are never indiscreet. Answers sometimes are.

—*Oscar Wilde*

Interviewing others is enjoyable if you determine ahead of time the basic questions you will ask. Good questions relate to the interests of the person you are interviewing. For example, you would not ask an eye doctor about foot care or an actress about politics.

Exercise #31

Pick a classmate to interview. Make a list of questions to ask that person (for example, his or her history, likes, dislikes, activities, hobbies, school, family). Keep your questions related to a central topic, and be as specific as possible. But allow for interesting sidetracks.

Interview the person for 10 minutes. Then allow yourself to be interviewed by someone.

_____

_____

_____

_____

_____

As a class, brainstorm a list of interview questions to ask your principal, guidance counselor, teacher, or other interesting people. From the list the class has come up with, write the best questions below in the order you would ask them. Use extra paper if necessary.

Principal

_____

_____

_____

_____

_____

Guidance counselor

_____

_____

_____

_____

_____

Teacher

_____

_____

_____

_____

_____

Another adult

_____

_____

_____

_____

_____

Putting It Together

Get together again with the person you interviewed, and ask him or her these questions:

▼ How did I do?

▼ Did I ask the right questions?

▼ How could I have done better?

▼ Was I an effective interviewer?

▼ Why or Why not?

Now, interview the adults you have chosen. Work in teams of two or three if possible. After the interview, discuss what you learned. Did you ask the right questions? What did you learn about others? What did you learn about yourself?

Activity 32.

Planning a Job Interview

Challenge

Unlike some interviewing experts, I believe that you should tell the truth in an interview.

–J. Michael Farr

The job interview is a crucial part of your job search. It usually is the first and only chance you have to make a good impression on a prospective employer. In Exercise #32, you'll practice the skills that will see you through your first and all of your job interviews.

Exercise #32

Assemble into small groups. Brainstorm a list of do's and don'ts for job interviews. Use the following list of factors to get you thinking.

▼ Leadership	▼ Maturity	▼ Appearance
▼ Manners	▼ Intelligence	▼ Attitude
▼ Posture	▼ Punctuality	▼ Alertness
▼ Enthusiasm	▼ Poise	▼ Speech
▼ Personality	▼ Education	▼ Originality
▼ Sincerity	▼ Training	▼ Experience

List the do's for a job applicant:

_____

_____

_____

_____

_____

List the don'ts for a job applicant:

_____

_____

_____

_____

_____

Putting It Together

In your small group, answer these questions:

▼ What kind of job do you want?

▼ What are your strengths, interests, training, and hobbies?

▼ How will these help you get the job?

Use your list of do's and don'ts to act out job interviews. Decide what job you are interviewing for; then have the others in your group play a committee interviewing you for the job. After you are interviewed, ask the committee to give you suggestions for a better interview.

Take turns until every member of the group has played the job applicant.

Activity 33.

Interviewing

Challenge

I was talking to a friend in a shop when a famous movie actress walked into the shop. I wanted to talk to the star—so I did. She was a person just like me and was just as fascinated that I wanted to talk with her as I was interested in talking to her.

Interviewing others is a skill anyone can develop. Most people love to talk about themselves, their families, and their work. The more you practice interviewing, the easier it will become. Soon, you'll find yourself wondering what you were nervous about in the first place!

Exercise #33

Use the dictionary to find the meanings for the following terms. Think about how you can weave these ideas into your interviewing style.

Recording (Note taking) _____

_____

Respect _____

_____

Ease _____

_____

Flow _____

_____

Tone _____

_____

Direction _____

_____

Choose one of the following people to interview:

▼ Family member   ▼ Politician   ▼ Crafts person

▼ Recreation leader   ▼ Neighbor   ▼ Business person

▼ Environmentalist   ▼ Social Security recipient   ▼ Other

Write down questions to ask this person. Arrange the questions in the order you want to ask them. Which question should you ask first? Which question do you want to ask next? What information is the most important to you?

1. _____

2. _____

3. _____

4. _____

5. _____

6. _____

Conduct your interview and write a paragraph or two describing the person you interviewed and his or her answers to your questions.

Putting It Together

In your small group, answer these questions:

▼ Before the interview, were you prepared?

▼ Did you feel self-conscious?

▼ After the interview, did you know the person better?

▼ Did your questions get the responses you wanted?

Discuss ways you could have made your questions better.

Activity 34.

Working Together

Challenge

They be blind leaders of the blind. And if the blind lead the blind, both shall fall into the ditch.

—The Bible, Matthew 15:14

To *cooperate* means to do a task together. Many jobs are done best by people working as a team. Each role in the team is important to complete the product. In this exercise, you'll work as a team to do a puzzle. Sound easy? Read on!

Exercise #34

Divide into groups of three to five. The teacher or group leader will tear a large sheet of paper into as many odd-shaped pieces as there are members. After tearing the pieces, the teacher will place a small square of adhesive tape on one side of each of the puzzle pieces.

One group at a time, each group should gather around three sides of a table in front of the class. Now for the fun part: Each person puts on a blindfold. After the blindfolds are in place, the teacher gives each person a part of the puzzle. Each group member, one at a time, must describe the puzzle piece by feeling its shape, the location of the tape, and the torn and smooth edges. If each person describes his or her puzzle piece accurately, the team should be able to put the puzzle together on the table.

Putting It Together

The task of the observers is to evaluate how well each group works together. Use the following form to make notes.

	Who took leadership?	Who followed well?	Who needed help in cooperation?	How would you do it better?
Group 1				
Group 2				
Group 3				
Group 4				

Activity 35.

Cooperation

Challenge

There's nothing is this world more instinctively abhorrent to me than finding myself in agreement with my fellow-humans.

—Malcolm Muggeridge

Cooperation is necessary when two or more people are called upon to make decisions. Your opinions and ideas are essential, and so is your willingness to hear another person's opinions and ideas. In this exercise, you'll think about cooperation, and how well you cooperate with others.

Exercise #35

What is "cooperation"? Define the word and give examples.

_____

_____

_____

List three characteristics of cooperative people.

1. _____

2. _____

3. _____

List three characteristics of uncooperative people.

1. _____

2. _____

3. _____

Look up the term "co-op." Give an example of such an enterprise.

_____

_____

_____

Define "corporation." How does that word relate to the word "cooperate"?

_____

_____

_____

Putting It Together

In your small groups, answer these questions:

▼ Are you cooperative?

▼ When is it easy to cooperate?

▼ When is it hard to cooperate?

▼ Are there certain people you cannot cooperate with? Why?

▼ Does cooperation mean giving up?

▼ Describe four times when cooperation was important in your life.

1. _____

2. _____

3. _____

4. _____

Activity 36.
Good "Followership"

Challenge

Being a good follower is just as important as being a good leader.

In our culture, we hear a lot about good leadership. When we elect a president, we ask, "Will that candidate provide strong, effective leadership?" But what about good "followership"? What does it mean to be a good follower?

Exercise #36

List three ways you acted as a follower in Exercises 34 and 35.

1. _____

2. _____

3. _____

Was your decision always a part of the final choice?

_____

How did that make you feel?

_____

Think of three other members of your group who are good followers. What makes them good followers?

1. _____

2. _____

3. _____

Was anyone in your group a poor follower? Why?

_____

_____

List three times when you were glad to be a follower.

1. _____

2. _____

3. _____

How is being a follower different from being a leader?

_____

How is it similar?

_____

Putting It Together

In your small groups, discuss these questions:

▼ Do you like being told what to do?

▼ Does it make a difference who is telling you what to do?

▼ Do you have a right to tell others what to do?

▼ Is there an effective way to get others to do what you want them to?

▼ As a group, make a list of history's most effective leaders. These can be people who led others to great good, or to evil. Leadership can work either way.

Activity 37.
You're the Boss

Challenge

You are the boss of a large clothing company. There are two job openings: one in the shipping department and one in the computer room. Eight people have applied for these two jobs. How do you know whom to hire?

Many people think being the boss is easy. After all, the boss just tells other people what to do all day. Right? In this exercise, you'll get a chance to "be the boss" and make some typical executive decisions.

Exercise #37

Your teacher will show you eight photos of people applying for a job. Whom would you choose for the job in the shipping department? Whom would you hire for the computer room? Circle *L* if you like the applicant at first glance, and *DL* if you don't like the applicant. Then, in the space at right, write *shipping* beside the name of the person you'd hire for the shipping department, and *computer* for the person you'd hire for the computer room:

Applicant's Name	Like/Dislike	Department
1. _____	L DL	_____
2. _____	L DL	_____
3. _____	L DL	_____
4. _____	L DL	_____
5. _____	L DL	_____
6. _____	L DL	_____
7. _____	L DL	_____
8. _____	L DL	_____

Look at each picture again. List one or two qualities you like or dislike about each person.

1. _____

2. _____

3. _____

4. _____

5. _____

6. _____

7. _____

8. _____

In the spaces below, write down why you picked the person you did for each department:

Shipping Department:

_____

_____

Computer Room:

_____

_____

Putting It Together

You just had to judge several people based only on their looks. How did you feel about that? In your small groups, discuss these questions:

▼ What turned you against some candidates?

▼ Did a person's eyes, mouth, expression, age, or gender matter in your decision?

▼ Are you judged by your looks?

▼ What do your eyes "say"?

▼ What does your posture say about you?

▼ How do you want people to judge you?

▼ Do you ever decide about a person by appearance only?

▼ Do you think you can recognize someone who is honest?

▼ Could you tell someone you should stay away from by appearance alone?

Activity 38.

Team Evaluation of Prospective Employees

Challenge

A good face they say, is a letter of recommendation. O Nature, Nature, why art thou so dishonest, as ever to send men with these false recommendations into the World!

—Henry Fielding

In this exercise, you'll combine your experience from Exercises 34, 35, 36, and 37. Your small group will be a company that must expand. As a team, you will determine the two new positions in your company and develop a complete, written job description of each position.

Exercise #38

Each member of your group should bring to class two pictures of ordinary people clipped from magazines or newspapers. One member shows one photo and briefly describes the person. The team's task is to decide whether to hire that person for one of the specific job openings you have. Each member should write his or her personal reasons (pro and con) and later share them.

Job Opening A

Title: _____

Duties and responsibilities: _____

Applicant	Hire?		Give Your Reasons
1. _____	Yes	No	_____
2. _____	Yes	No	_____
3. _____	Yes	No	_____

	Hire?		Give Your Reasons
4. _____	Yes	No	_____
5. _____	Yes	No	_____
6. _____	Yes	No	_____
7. _____	Yes	No	_____
8. _____	Yes	No	_____

Job Opening B

Title: _____

Duties and responsibilities: _____

Applicant	Hire?		Give Your Reasons
1. _____	Yes	No	_____
2. _____	Yes	No	_____
3. _____	Yes	No	_____
4. _____	Yes	No	_____
5. _____	Yes	No	_____
6. _____	Yes	No	_____
7. _____	Yes	No	_____
8. _____	Yes	No	_____

Putting It Together

What qualities do bosses want? Do you have them? What makes you already successful—even if you don't have the special job training for some jobs? What is your attitude? In your small groups, discuss these questions, and those that follow:

▼ When have you been judged poorly?

▼ What did you do to lead someone to a poor judgment of you?

▼ Could you have done anything differently?

▼ Can you change the other person's judgment of you?

Now compare and discuss your decisions about each applicant. Answer these questions:

▼ Are first judgments ever wrong? When?

▼ What can you tell from a person's face or body? From a person's clothes or hair?

▼ Is it fair to judge a person at first glance?

▼ What is an "attitude"?

▼ What attitudes do employers want?

▼ What happened when you tried to convince the others in your group to hire an applicant you liked but they didn't?

Activity 39.

Discussions and Debates

Challenge

Freedom is hammered out on the anvil of discussion, dissent, and debate.

—Hubert H. Humphrey

There are formal procedures you can follow for presenting your opinions and ideas to groups. Some of these formal methods are questioning experts, pro-con debates, and presentation/feedback. In this exercise, you'll get a chance to try out all three methods.

Exercise #39

Questioning Experts

In "expert questioning," you seek information by asking questions of an expert. You should prepare your questions in advance to ensure a smoother flow of information.

Your small group will divide into the following roles to demonstrate this method of presentation to the total group.

Questioners: _____

Experts: _____

Moderator: _____

You will be asked about a special hobby or interest you have. Remember that if you talk about something you enjoy, your attitude will make the presentation interesting. If you don't know an answer, you should say so without embarrassment.

List a special hobby or interest on which you consider yourself an expert:

_____

_____

_____

Pro-Con Debate

In a pro-con debate, different sides of the same issue are represented by experts. Someone may take an opposing view to provide interest in the discussion and to learn about the opposing view.

State an opinion you hold strongly: _____

_____

Again, assume roles and present your opinions to the total group.

Presentation/Feedback

One expert presents information to the audience and then answers questions.

Do you have an area of interest that you can describe to the class? _____

_____

Make an "expert" presentation to the total group.

Putting It Together

Evaluate three of the class's presentations below:

	Questioning Experts	Pro-Con Debate	Presentation/ Feedback
Were the arguments convincing?			
Did the presenter research the topic adequately?			
Did he or she include pertinent aspects of the topic?			
Was the team well-organized?			
Did they listen to the opposing side's argument?			
What was the overall impression of the presentation?			

Offer some suggestions for improvement.

Activity 40.

Vote on It

Challenge

The ignorance of one voter in a democracy impairs the security of all.

—John F. Kennedy

Groups often make decisions by voting for or against an issue. A decision you make alone involves only one vote—yours. If you and another person must decide an issue, there are two votes. In a democracy, the people agree to abide by the decisions voted for by the majority of the population. In this exercise, you'll get to vote on some issues.

Exercise #40

Define and give examples of the following voting terms:

Compromise: _____

_____

_____

Alternative: _____

_____

_____

Majority: _____

_____

_____

Minority: _____

_____

_____

Persuasion: _____

_____

_____

Filibuster: _____

_____

_____

You can arrive at group decisions in several ways. Give an example of each of the following terms and where it may be used:

Secret ballot: _____

_____

_____

Open ballot: _____

_____

_____

Roll call: _____

_____

_____

Consensus: _____

_____

_____

Opinion survey: _____

_____

_____

SECTION 2: SUCCESS WITH OTHERS

Others (list): _____

_____

_____

Putting It Together

In your small group, devise a ballot that requires the decision of the whole class.

Think of three different issues for the class to vote on. Write them in the spaces below.

▼ Issue #1 _____

▼ Issue #2 _____

▼ Issue #3 _____

Make a ballot for each issue, and hand out the ballots to the entire class. Have everyone vote, fold their ballots, and turn them in. Now tally the vote.

Outcome

	# of Votes	% of Votes
Issue #1		
Issue #2		
Issue #3		

What percentage of votes is required to win? Does it differ with issues or people? From place to place? Discuss the differences.

Activity 41.

Be an Expert

Challenge

An expert "double-talker" was hired to fool the professionals at a recent national conference. He knew nothing about his topic but could invent words and concepts and talk for hours. The audience rated him as the best and most knowledgeable speaker of the conference.

You may be a "double-talking" expert. It takes more than just brains—it takes nerve! In this exercise, you'll get a chance to try your hand at "faking your way through a topic." How good are you at blarney?

Exercise #41

Be bold! Pick a subject you know nothing about, and then be specific. For example, don't merely talk about space. Give your topic as "the Function of Columbia's Inertial Guidance System on Suborbital Flights."

Write your specific "expert" subject here: _____

You have three minutes to be an expert in front of the class. You will give a short introduction and answer questions from the audience. Give "expert" answers, even if you don't know what you are talking about. Make up answers, words, and ideas. Convince the class you know what you are talking about.

Oh, yes, I almost forgot: You will be given your topic by a classmate as you get to the front of the room. The topic you picked is to be given to someone else.

Keep in mind an old adage: "Prepare for 10 hours to speak well for 10 minutes. Prepare for 10 minutes to speak poorly for 10 hours."

Putting It Together

In your small groups, rate one another's presentations. How well did each of you do at bluffing your way through a topic you knew nothing about? Discuss these questions:

▼ Who in our society uses double-talk and makes a living at it?

▼ How can you tell when someone is bluffing?

▼ When might bluffing be a valuable tool to you?

▼ When might it get you into trouble?

Activity 42.
Evaluating Experts

Challenge

"X" means "unknown." A "spurt" is a drip under pressure. Thus, an "X-spurt" is "an unknown drip under pressure."

One of the greatest challenges of living in a democracy is judging the experts. Who are the real experts? Who are the bluffers? It's not always easy to tell, as you may have discovered in Exercise #41. In this exercise, you'll evaluate who in your class did well at bluffing, and try to determine what made that person good. Are there cues to look for? What can tell you if a person is bluffing? And how can you become better at being a "real" expert, presenting the material you do know in a professional, believable way?

Exercise #42

Name three persons in your class who were good at "experting." What were their expert qualities?

Person	Qualities
1.	
2.	
3.	

What do you know most about? (Don't be humble or shy here.) What have you studied or found the most interesting? Be specific.

_____

_____

_____

Do you want to learn more or spend time doing this? _____

Write some ideas on how you can put more time or energy into what you are interested in:

_____

_____

_____

Do others know about these interests? _____

Who else knows enough to help you in this area of "expertise"?

_____

_____

How can they help? Be specific.

_____

_____

_____

 # Putting It Together

In your small group, discuss the following questions:

▼ Do you like letting others know what you are good at?

▼ What is your usual method of gaining respect?

▼ Does it work for you?

▼ Where can you improve on your presentation of yourself?

▼ What can you do to become more of an "expert" in your chosen field?

▼ Who can you ask for help in your quest for knowledge and proficiency?

▼ What *is* proficiency?

Share your interests with others in your group. Trade ideas on how to make your proficiencies better known.

Activity 43.
The Decision-Making Process

Challenge

I have just decided not to write a Challenge for you.

We all make decisions every day. Should you have cereal or a bagel for breakfast? Should you wear jeans or sweats to school? Should you pay attention in class or take a nap. Life is full of decisions. Some are small and don't really affect much else, but some are intimidating and hard to make. How do you make decisions? Do you have a method, or do you just react to other people's choices?

Are there times when you don't have any options to decide from? Remember this: *You always decide how you will react in any situation.*

Exercise #43

Action		Option
Action A	Action B	Neither option looks good.
Action A	Obstacle	Choose to get around, over, or under the obstacle.
Action A	Action B	Both choices look good.
Action dictated		No choice looks possible.

Give an example of a choice you had to make when neither option looked good.

_____

_____

Share an experience when you had to overcome an obstacle in order to take the right action.

_____

_____

How do you choose when both options look good?

_____

_____

What options do you have when you can't see any options?

_____

_____

 # Putting It Together

In your small group, discuss the following questions:

▼ What do you do if it looks like you can do nothing?

▼ When does this happen in your life?

▼ Is doing nothing a valid choice sometimes?

Read the following scenario; then brainstorm a list of options (the wilder the better) a person in this situation might consider:

Case Study

Terry Anderson was held hostage in Lebanon for seven years. Often shackled and blindfolded, he was held in solitary confinement, beaten, threatened with death, and did not know if he would ever make it home again. He had no control over even the basics in life: where he was, what or when he would eat, when he would stand or sit, what he would wear.

What options did Terry Anderson have? Well, only he could decide how he would respond to his captors. Only he could decide whether to give up or go on hoping. His captors could control his body, but they could not control his mind, his spirit, and his will.

We may not always like the situations we find ourselves in, but we always get the choice of how to respond.

Activity 44.

Live Life or Be Run by It

Challenge

> *No man is good enough to govern another man without that other's consent.*
>
> —*Abraham Lincoln*

Can you imagine a horse walking down the street, pushing a cart in front of it? Can you picture your life being controlled by everyone or everything around you? That's as ridiculous as a cart-drawn horse.

Exercise #44

List four areas in which you have only a limited voice in decision making:

1. _____

2. _____

3. _____

4. _____

Now decide which two of these areas most concern you. List some ways you would like to take more responsibility in these areas:

1. _____

2. _____

Putting It Together

Share one or two areas of decision making over which you feel you have little control, and what you plan to do about it. Can you do it gently but firmly?

Discuss these questions as a group:

▼ How does it feel when you gain control of your own life?

▼ When does it happen?

▼ What can you do when someone you love is trying to control your life?

▼ Is there a difference between being a good follower and being controlled?

▼ Is confrontation bad?

Activity 45.
Remembering

Challenge

A man's real possession is his memory. In nothing else is he rich, in nothing else is he poor.

—Alexander Smith

Storing information in your brain is easy. The hard part is pulling the information out of storage. It takes practice to be able to retrieve specific data or pictures on command. In this exercise, you'll work on your memory skills.

Exercise #45

Read the following paragraph once; then cover it up and answer the questions that follow *without looking at the paragraph again*.

The fires in the log and bark-covered longhouse threw flickering shadows on the carved masks of the false faces. These men of the solemn wooden countenances had danced around and through the fires for a day and two nights. The observers on the benches surrounding this tribal ritual had the glazed and entranced looks of those who look too long into the fire.

—*from the novel Holy Savages, by Dennis Hooker*

1. Are the dancers Native Americans?

_____

2. What material are the masks made from?

_____

3. Give the writer's first name.

_____

Was it easy or hard to remember the details? With practice, you will find you can remember more than you think. Some learning experts recommend reading out loud to increase the amount you retain. Another method, called *paraphrasing*, involves reading the material silently, then closing your eyes and saying aloud *in your own words* what the material was about.

Another memory method is to relate what you are learning to something you already know. For example, say you know how to make chocolate chip cookies. And now you are reading the directions for peanut butter cookies. One way to remember the directions is to look for similarities in the new recipe and the one you know. Then you have to learn only the differences.

Putting It Together

Write your own "factual paragraph" (make up the facts, if you want to).

Your paragraph will be read to your small group for a "TV game show." Write 10 questions to ask the contestants. (Be accurate.)

1. _____

2. _____

3. _____

4. _____

5. _____

6. _____

7. _____

8. _____

9. _____

10. _____

You are the game show host. Your group members are the contestants. Read your paragraph and ask your questions. See who answers the most questions correctly and quickly. Take turns playing the host and the contestants.

Activity 46.
Your Classmates

Challenge

I think your whole life shows in your face and you should be proud of that.

—Lauren Bacall

Can you tell what a person is like by looking at her? Can you tell what a person is thinking or feeling by looking at him? There's an old saying: You can't tell a book by its cover … but you can tell how it has been used.

Exercise #46

Note: In this exercise, you will need to be gentle and sensitive. Humor is not appropriate here. Remember, you are writing about others, while others are writing about you.

Look at four people across the room from you. Decide what each is thinking and feeling. Fill in the chart below.

Name	What is the person thinking about?	What does the person usually feel?	How did you know these things?
1.			
2.			
3.			
4.			

Look at each of these classmates again. What more would you like to know about each of them?

1. _____

2. _____

3. _____

4. _____

Putting It Together

In your small group, discuss these questions:

▼ What are the joys and hazards of getting close to others?

▼ Why would you want to know more about others?

▼ Is it easy to really know someone else? Why or why not?

▼ Do you want others to know you? Why or why now?

Activity 47.
Using Graphic Words

Challenge

You've probably heard the old expression, "A picture is worth a thousand words." But have you heard this one? "One word can trigger a thousand pictures."

Graphic words flash a visual image on the screen of your understanding. For example, what picture comes to mind when you hear the word *ooze*? How about *plush*? What about *healthy*? Words can evoke pictures or sounds or memories. Graphic words are powerful tools for communicating who you are to others.

Exercise #47

Read the message below. What does it say about the author?

Now write a "hieroglyphics" message about yourself in the space below.

Putting It Together

Ask the members of your group to read your message. Can they decipher it? Do they have suggestions to improve it?

Working as a group, make a hieroglyphics message from the paragraph below. Use scrap paper for the preliminary work; then write the final product in the space provided.

Case Study

When I graduate, I want to work in a job that is challenging and fun. As long as I like my job, I am successful. I will not worry about other people's ideas of success. I will accept responsibility for making my own choices. I will accept the credit for my own success.

Now make a list of words that can be drawn as pictures. These are powerful, graphic words—words that evoke visual images. Use them often as you write or talk.

_____

_____

_____

_____

_____

Activity 48.
Feelings List

Challenge

The only questions worth asking today are whether humans are going to have any emotions tomorrow, and what the quality of life will be if the answer is no.

—Lester Bangs

Feelings are powerful things in humans. Wars have been fought, lives have been lost, and great sacrifices have been made because of emotions like fear, anger, and love. Feelings can lead us to great good or to dreadful wrongs. When we are joyous, we feel we could rule the world. When we're in the depths of depression, we think we might not make it through another day. We are a feeling people, and our experiences of feelings are a common bond. Black or white, male or female, old or young, rich or poor, we all feel pain when we are betrayed, joy when we are loved, and fear when we are threatened.

Exercise #48

Underline the feelings you have experienced in your life. In the space beside each item, write the initial of someone you know who shares that feeling.

___ Abandoned	___ Bitter	___ Condemned
___ Adequate	___ Bold	___ Confused
___ Affectionate	___ Bored	___ Conspicuous
___ Agonized	___ Brave	___ Contented
___ Almighty	___ Burdened	___ Creative
___ Ambivalent		___ Cruel
___ Angry	___ Calm	___ Crushed
___ Annoyed	___ Capable	
___ Anxious	___ Challenged	___ Deceitful
___ Apathetic	___ Charmed	___ Defeated
___ Astounded	___ Cheated	___ Delighted
___ Awed	___ Cheerful	___ Despairing
	___ Childish	___ Destructive
___ Bad	___ Clever	___ Determined
___ Beautiful	___ Combative	___ Different
___ Betrayed	___ Competitive	___ Discontented

___ Distracted
___ Disturbed
___ Divided
___ Dominated
___ Doubtful

___ Electrified
___ Empty
___ Enchanted
___ Energetic
___ Envious
___ Evil
___ Excited
___ Exhausted

___ Fascinated
___ Fearful
___ Flustered
___ Foolish
___ Frantic
___ Free
___ Frightened
___ Frustrated
___ Furious

___ Glad
___ Good
___ Gratified
___ Greedy
___ Guilty

___ Happy
___ Hateful
___ Heavenly
___ Helpful
___ Helpless
___ High
___ Homesick
___ Honored
___ Horrible
___ Hurt
___ Hysterical

___ Ignored
___ Impressed
___ Infuriated
___ Inspired

___ Intimidated
___ Isolated

___ Jealous
___ Joyous
___ Jumpy

___ Keen
___ Kind

___ Lazy
___ Left out
___ Lonely
___ Longing
___ Low
___ Lustful

___ Mad
___ Mean
___ Melancholy
___ Miserable
___ Mystical

___ Nervous
___ Nice
___ Nutty

___ Obnoxious
___ Obsessed
___ Odd
___ Opposed
___ Outraged
___ Overwhelmed

___ Pained
___ Panicked
___ Peaceful
___ Persecuted
___ Pitiful
___ Pleased
___ Pressured
___ Pretty
___ Proud

___ Quarrelsome

___ Refreshed

___ Rejected
___ Relaxed
___ Relieved
___ Remorseful
___ Restless
___ Reverent
___ Rewarded
___ Righteous

___ Sad
___ Satisfied
___ Scared
___ Screwed
___ Settled
___ Sexy
___ Shocked
___ Silly
___ Skeptical
___ Sneaky
___ Solemn
___ Sorrowful
___ Spiteful
___ Startled
___ Stingy
___ Stunned
___ Suffering
___ Sure
___ Sympathetic

___ Tempted
___ Tense
___ Terrible
___ Threatened
___ Tired
___ Trapped
___ Troubled

___ Ugly
___ Uneasy
___ Unsettled

___ Vicious

___ Weepy
___ Wicked
___ Wonderful
___ Worried

Putting It Together

In your small group, discuss these questions:

▼ Which is the most powerful emotion?

▼ Which emotion is at the root of most violence: hate, love, anger, or fear?

▼ Is it possible to feel something no one else has ever felt before?

▼ What is the most powerful emotion you have experienced?

▼ What is the most common emotion you experience?

Activity 49.
Feelings Bingo

Challenge

The young man who has not wept is a savage, and the old man who will not laugh is a fool.

—*George Santayana*

Most people have a hard time identifying their feelings. Indeed, feelings are hard to pinpoint. What we call a "feeling" is actually a sensory response to an internal or external event. We learn to think in terms of feelings like "good," "bad," "happy," and "sad." But there are hundreds of subtle variations of feelings.

For example, you can be sad, or you can be depressed, morose, sorrowful, lonely, or in despair. You can be happy; you also can be elated, joyous, exhilarated, enchanted, delighted, or charmed. You can be angry, or you can be irritated, furious, enraged, or annoyed.

In this exercise, you will use the feelings you chose in Exercise #48 to play an adaptation of Bingo.

Exercise #49

From the feelings list in Exercise #48, choose feelings you have had yourself and put one in each of the squares of game 1 below. Your teacher will select words at random from the feelings list and say them out loud. If the feeling he or she calls matches one you listed on your game square, put an "X" through that box. When you have three in a row (down, across, or at an angle), you have a "Bingo."

Game 1

1	2	3
4	5	6
7	8	9

Game 2

1	2	3
4	5	6
7	8	9

Game 3

1	2	3
4	5	6
7	8	9

Game 4

1	2	3
4	5	6
7	8	9

Activity 50.

The Sponge

Challenge

A sponge opens to soak up water. A clam clamps closed to shut out the world. A person who is being complimented should be like a sponge—not a clam.

It's hard for most of us to accept compliments. Someone compliments our hair. "Oh, it's a mess today," we say.

They like our outfit. "This old thing?"

They think we're smart. "Not really," we answer. "I stink in algebra."

It seems easier to accept criticism than admiration, but we all crave acceptance and admiration. In this exercise, you'll write compliments about other people and think about how you respond when people compliment you.

Exercise #50

Pretend you are talking directly to the people listed below. Say two honest, positive things about each person. Imagine that each enjoys what you say and soaks up your compliments like a sponge.

Person	Positive Statement
A parent	1.
	2.
Another close relative	1.
	2.
A female friend	1.
	2.

Person	Positive Statement
A male friend	1.
	2.
An instructor/teacher	1.
	2.
Someone you don't really like	1.
	2.

Putting It Together

In your small group, discuss these questions:

▼ How do you feel when you think positively about people you know?

▼ How do you feel when you spend time thinking negatively about people?

▼ Are you positive or negative most of the time?

▼ Are there times when it's okay to think negatively?

Now, go to some of the people you listed above and share your positive thoughts with them. Accept the positive sharing of others as you would want them to accept yours.

Activity 51.

Working with Others: Seeds of Service 2

Challenge

My fellow Americans, ask not what your country can do for you—ask what you can do for your country.

—*John F. Kennedy*

In Section 1 of this book, you listed ways you can increase your service to the world. It may be that no great or earth-shattering ideas have occurred to you yet. You may not see a hidden gem in your ideas for years to come.

Imagining how you can help others in your community and the world will be necessary many times in your life because your ideas grow and your life changes.

Exercise #51

Again using the brainstorming technique, jot down ways you can work with others to help those in your community and the world.

_____

_____

_____

_____

_____

_____

_____

Putting It Together

Share your ideas with your small group. Remember, no judgments or snickering is allowed. How can you work with others to help even more people? Work as a group to brainstorm a list of ideas.

Discuss the following questions:

▼ Do you prefer to work alone or in a group (such as with a church or charity organization) to help in your community?

▼ How can you help people in other parts of the world?

▼ Is it easier to help others or to receive help from others?

▼ Do you have a responsibility for other people in your community?

Simulation 2:
The Business

In this section of the book, you have shared your thoughts and feelings with others in your small groups and in the large group. You have talked with others, made individual and group decisions, and heard the feelings of other members as they have heard yours. And you have planned and completed projects alone and with others.

You have gone beyond your own uniqueness to realize your similarities with others: the emotions you share, the experiences you have in common. You have been successful as your communication skills increased with your friends and team members. In this simulation, you will make good use of those communication skills.

In Simulation 1, your group produced a successful game. In this simulation, you will organize your team into a company to produce and sell your game to others.

By now, you know the other members of your team and their areas of interest and expertise. Keep these in mind as you decide on who should fill various jobs in your business, such as president, secretary, treasurer, bookkeeper, and marketing specialists. Make a *workable* organization. You will decide on the following things:

▼ How to finance the business. Where will the money come from? Will you take a loan from the bank? Will you take on investors?

▼ The market. Who will buy your game? Where is your market? How will you reach that market?

▼ What price to charge. How much will it cost to produce your game? How much do you need to charge to cover your expenses? How much profit do you want to make?

▼ Other important issues. How will the game be produced? How much money will each member of the team make? Will the president receive a higher salary than the bookkeeper?

Time Passes ...

Your organization is up and running; your product is selling well. In fact, your business is so successful you need outside help to expand. Now you will try to recruit members from other teams. Have your group interview people from other teams. Phrase your interview questions so that you see each person's strong points.

You must hire two qualified people to help your company. What positions do you need to fill? List the skills and training you are seeking in a new employee for each position.

Even More Time Passes …

The demand for your game is good, but not overwhelming. You decide to combine your game with that of another team: you're going to do *a merger*. Decide before you meet what is necessary to do business with another company. Do you have weak areas you need to strengthen? Could your games be similar? Plan the criteria for meeting and doing business with this company for the proposed merger.

Meet with the other small groups, exchanging proposals for the mergers. Decide on the company you'll merge with. How will you handle it if another company also wants to merge with the company you choose. Will you negotiate with that company, make a better offer, or look around for a different one?

Evaluating

What are the next steps you would take if you were to take this project to an actual corporation to market your game in the real world? Discuss the feasibility of actually selling your game. Do you believe in your product? In your organization? If not, why not?

Small Group Inventory 2

Now that you have completed the second simulation in this book, take a few minutes to write down your opinions of the small group you have been working with. Think carefully about how your group worked together. (Complete the form individually.)

Characteristic	Low	Average	High
1. Level of sincerity			
You all tried to do your best	1	2	3
You all attempted to learn more	1	2	3
Comments			

Characteristic	Low	Average	High
2. Research			
Used many sources	1	2	3
Clear, straightforward sharing of material	1	2	3
Comments			
3. Awareness			
You attempted to listen to the ideas of others	1	2	3
Level at which the group communicates ideas	1	2	3
Comments			
4. Cooperation			
Level at which you worked together	1	2	3
You tried to understand the needs of others	1	2	3
Comments			
5. Product			
You completed your work	1	2	3
Clarity of work	1	2	3
Appearance of work	1	2	3
Comments			
6. Your Overall Satisfaction with the Group	1	2	3
Comments			

Self-Inventory 2

Now evaluate yourself. How are you doing so far? Before you begin answering these questions, review your responses in Section 2 and what you have learned about yourself.

Ask yourself these questions honestly and with a fair degree of self-examination.

Characteristic	Low	Average	High
1. My Level of Sincerity			
I desired to do my best	1	2	3
I attempted to learn more	1	2	3
I tried to cooperate	1	2	3
2. My Research			
I used many sources	1	2	3
I wrote clear, straightforward responses in book	1	2	3
I tried to find more resources	1	2	3
3. My Awareness of Myself			
I discovered new things	1	2	3
I tried to improve	1	2	3
I worked on personal challenges	1	2	3
4. My Awareness of Others			
I cooperated in my group	1	2	3
Level of my ability to communicate ideas	1	2	3
My ability to assist others	1	2	3
5. My Written and Oral Product			
Quality of my oral report	1	2	3
Excellence of my written work	1	2	3
Amount of preparation for oral or written work	1	2	3

Characteristic	Low	Average	High
6. Carryover Outside School			
Homework	1	2	3
Degree of interest in my studies	1	2	3
Hobbies and interests that relate to this course	1	2	3
7. My Overall Sense of Personal Satisfaction			
My satisfaction with my personal growth	1	2	3
My ability to be a friend	1	2	3
My awareness of the world	1	2	3
Amount of available energy I used	1	2	3
Degree I progressed compared to my potential	1	2	3

Moving On

Having completed two sections of this book, you know much more about yourself and about the group you have been working with. Working through this section of the book and the simulation *The Business*, you have discovered how you work within your group and the unique gifts you bring to it.

In Section 3, you will see how successful you can be as you take your talents and those of your group to the world around you.

You may be surprised to find out that the world will see you and your group as successful. As you go through Section 3, you will find success you may not have known before—the success of making a difference in the world.

Don't forget, there are no "right" or "wrong" answers here, only differences of opinion!

Your Success in the World

Section 1 of this book helped you learn more about yourself. In Section 2, you shared experiences with other people in your groups. In Section 3, you will look outside yourself and your group into the world. This is a world that *needs you* and what you can offer. At the same time, you can learn even more about yourself as you stretch your imagination even further.

As you have learned, success is merely the path you are on when you decide that you are important. You don't have to compare yourself with others to be successful. Even "winning" and "losing" are not important to being successful. Section 3 should show you that you don't have to prove yourself to anyone else.

In this section, you will work toward the final simulation, called *The Communiqué*. This simulation will have you develop a newsletter to the world and will bring together all you have learned in the earlier two sections of the book.

The Communiqué gives you the ultimate challenge to share yourself, your ideas, your creativity, your concern, and your caring with the world.

Activity 52.

Design Your Own Evaluation

Challenge

Everyone receives grades or some form of evaluation in school and on the job. Until now you've had no voice in how you are evaluated. Now you do.

Have you ever griped about a grade you received? Do you think the grading system your teachers use doesn't show what you do well? In this exercise, you will design your own report card based on your own grading system. What is important to show on the card? What information should the card include? It's all up to you.

Exercise #52

Working in small groups, brainstorm ideas for a new report card. Remember, in brainstorming anything goes. The person recording the ideas should write them all down—even the outlandish ones. You'll revise later; for now, just let your imaginations run wild.

What we want to evaluate:

_____

_____

_____

The best way to design the evaluation card:

_____

_____

_____

Now, as a group, make a first draft of your card, including the best ideas from your brainstorming list. Exchange your group's card with other small groups.

This is the time it's okay to steal ideas from your classmates! Read through the lists from other groups. In the space below, list the other ideas you want to include in your own evaluation. Share your constructive criticisms with the other groups about their cards.

_____

_____

Working individually now, write up a finished report card for yourself.

_____

_____

List the best assets of your report card:

1. _____

2. _____

3. _____

4. _____

5. _____

6. _____

Putting It Together

Get together again with your small group. Have each member of the group present his or her card and explains its benefits. Do you all have different cards now, or are some of the cards alike? Discuss the following questions:

▼ How do the differences in your cards reflect your own differences in perspective and interests?

▼ Can you all agree on one card that accurately reflects all of you?

▼ Could a teacher use your card to fairly grade the entire class?

Working as a group again, combine the best elements from each card into one group grading card:

_____

Activity 53.
Sharing Your Interests

Challenge

One half of the world cannot understand the pleasures of the other.

—Jane Austen

Your interests are uniquely yours. What you love to do is shaped by who you are and what you have done before. You may be interested in music, art, sports, or construction. Perhaps you want to help people, learn about foreign places, understand machines, or make lots of money. Your interests say a lot about you and can point toward a future career. In this exercise, you'll explore ways to pursue your interests individually and in your community.

Exercise #53

List two of your major interests:

1._____

2._____

Where in your community can you get more experience or training in your area of interest? (You can ask around or look in the *Yellow Pages* to find more information on this.)

_____

_____

_____

How can you become better at your interests?

_____

_____

_____

Putting It Together

One of your interests may be marketable—you may be able to make money at it now or in the future. Are there ways to make one of your interests pay for itself now?

In your small group, brainstorm ways to start your own clubs for your interests. Take turns looking at each person's interests and brainstorming lists. Each person should write down his or her own list.

_____

_____

_____

_____

Working individually now, go back and think about each idea you wrote down.

Now rank the ideas on your list.

_____

_____

_____

_____

_____

_____

Devise a plan to initiate one of your ideas.

_____

_____

_____

_____

Activity 54.

Unwritten Words

Challenge

What I like in a good author isn't what he says, but what he whispers.

—*Logan Pearsall Smith*

Have you heard the expression, "The best stories are written between the lines"? That old saying echoes the cardinal rule of good writing: Show me, don't tell me. In this exercise, you'll have a chance to do some creative writing. You will write short story to evoke a feeling.

Exercise #54

Decide what feelings you want your reader to have after reading your story. List those feelings on the dotted lines below. On the solid lines, write words that will evoke those feelings.

_____

- -

_____

- -

_____

- -

_____

- -

Now choose one feeling. (Be creative; use the list of feelings from Section 2 to spark ideas of different feelings.) Think of a scene that is sure to leave the reader with that feeling, and write it in the space below.

_____

_____

_____

Use a separate sheet to write a one-page scene. Work on it until you feel confident the reader will develop a specific feeling during or after reading your scene.

Putting It Together

Do you have a good story? What, if anything, does it need? Does it give your readers the feeling you want them to have?

Get into groups of three and share your stories. Ask your readers to tell you the feelings they have when reading your story.

▼ Reader #1

▼ Reader #2

▼ Did you get the reaction you wanted?

▼ Ask for suggestions to make the scene even better. List eight suggestions below.

1. _____

2. _____

3. _____

4. _____

5. _____

6. _____

7. _____

8. _____

Activity 55.
The Courtroom

Challenge

It may be true that the law cannot make a man love me, but it can keep him from lynching me, and I think that's pretty important.

—Martin Luther King, Jr.

Do you know the expression "Justice is blind"? It means that justice should be the same for all people, rich or poor, black or white, powerful and meek. The laws of the land should be the same for all the people of the land. That is the ideal of the American judicial system.

In exercise #55, you will be the judicial system to get an inside look at how the courts work.

Exercise #55

In groups of at least eight, decide who will play each of the following roles:

▼ **Judge:** The judge makes sure things run fairly. His or her decision is final.

▼ **Prosecuting Attorney:** The prosecutor's job is to convince the jury that the accused is guilty.

▼ **Defense Attorney:** The defense attorney must convince the jury that the accused is innocent.

▼ **Defendant:** This is the person accused of the crime.

▼ **Plaintiff:** Sometimes called the victim, this is the person accusing the defendant of committing the crime.

▼ **Jury:** The jury must decide whether the defendant is guilty or not guilty.

Choose a crime. Be very specific. Try to find a crime in which the sides are not clear-cut. For example, you might try a case in which the state (the plaintiff) is suing parents (the defendants) for not seeking medical care for their children because of their religious beliefs. Or one in which the school board (the plaintiff) is confronting a 15-year-old (the defendant) for not attending school because she is working to help support her family after her father is laid off from his job. You get the idea. Brainstorm for the most interesting crime.

Allow time for the plaintiff and prosecuting attorney to brainstorm their case. At the same time, the defendant and defense attorney should brainstorm their defense.

Next, arrange your desks and chairs to resemble a courtroom and try the case.

Putting It Together

After each group presents its trial, the class should discuss all aspects of the case. List suggestions for a better trial. Now, try another case.

Activity 56.
Two Sides to an Argument

Challenge

The difficult part in an argument is not to defend one's opinion, but rather to know it.

—André Maurois

Sometimes, in order to maintain your integrity, you must take a definite moral and ethical stand. Other decisions are not so clear-cut. In our multicultural society, you will continually meet people whose beliefs are different from yours. And throughout your life, you will have to decide whether those differences are acceptable or not. Some you may decide you can live with. For example, someone else being a vegetarian while you eat meat may be an acceptable difference. Others, you may feel compelled to stand publicly against.

These are decisions you will have to make again and again throughout your life. In this exercise, you'll start thinking about where you stand on a few issues.

Exercise #56

Mark where you stand on the following statements:

	Strongly Agree	Not Sure	Strongly Disagree
Gifts are not appreciated as much as something we earn.	❑	❑	❑
Men and women think differently.	❑	❑	❑
School is a necessity of life.	❑	❑	❑
A person should achieve independence by the time he or she is 20.	❑	❑	❑
The government should stay out of people's lives as much as possible.	❑	❑	❑

	Strongly Agree	Not Sure	Strongly Disagree
The government should provide a safety net for the poor.	❏	❏	❏
Two can live more cheaply than one.	❏	❏	❏
The world is becoming a better place.	❏	❏	❏
An important issue of your choice:			
An important issue of your choice:			

Putting It Together

In this activity, you will dramatize your moral or ethical stand.

1. A moderator will read a statement. Those who strongly agree with the statement will stand on the moderator's right; those who strongly disagree will stand on the left. Those who aren't sure will stand in the middle.

2. The students standing to the moderator's right (the "pros") get five minutes to convince the others of their way of thinking. Next, the students to the left (the "cons") get five minutes to convince the others of their way of thinking. After both groups have had their turns, the "not sures" must take a stand as pros or cons. Pros and cons may switch sides if they decide differently.

3. The moderator will read another statement, and students again are to move to the right if they agree, or to the left if they don't. (This time, no one can remain in the middle.)

4. Each group again gets five minutes to convince the others, only this time they will argue the opposite side of the case. That is, the pros will argue against the statement, the cons will argue for it, even though they don't really believe it.

Assemble in your small groups. Try to come to a consensus on each of the issues listed in Exercise #56. Can you? What alternatives do you have?

Finally, as a class, take a vote on the issues. List the results on the board.

Activity 57.

Learning Modes

Challenge

A school is not a factory. Its raison d'être is to provide opportunity for experience.

—*J. L. Carr*

We become not a melting pot but a beautiful mosaic. Different people, different beliefs, different yearnings, different hopes, different dreams.

—*Jimmy Carter*

Students usually are taught in school through sight or hearing. That's why persons with poor vision or hearing can easily become poor students. But each of us is able to learn in many other ways.

The easiest teaching method, of course, is simply to stand at the front of the class and lecture. But the best teachers are able to teach the same idea in many different ways. In this exercise, you will get the chance to prepare a lesson using other teaching methods.

Exercise #57

Some people learn by hearing; some by reading; some by watching; some by doing. Some people retain knowledge better if they set it to music. Many people combine several methods to learn. In this exercise, you will divide into groups of "specialists" in different learning modes, including these:

▼ **Visual learning:** Learning by reading, watching videos, demonstrations, etc.

▼ **Audio learning:** Learning by hearing lectures, music, videos, etc.

▼ **Kinesthetic learning:** Learning by touching, participating, performing a task, etc.

▼ **Combination learning:** Learning that combines several senses

Each group of specialists will prepare a lesson on a topic of your choosing. After you have chosen a topic, answer the following questions:

How do you begin your research?

_____

_____

_____

List some places you can find this information:

_____

_____

_____

Name two outside "specialists" who can help you gather information:

1. _____

2. _____

Brainstorm with your group to come up with new ways to teach the idea or a concept, using the learning style you chose.

_____

_____

_____

Finally, each group is to present a lesson on its topic, using the learning mode it chose.

Putting It Together

In your small groups, discuss these questions:

▼ What are your strongest learning modalities?

▼ What is your weakest?

▼ How have you been taught in the past?

▼ How can you improve your learning ability?

▼ How can you find out more about this area?

Activity 58.
Body Talk

Challenge

Nothing is more revealing than movement.

—Martha Graham

You usually let the world know what you think by the words you say. But you also send messages by the way you stand, move your arms, and hold your head. The expression on your face speaks volumes by itself. If you don't believe it, try this: In a crowded place, pick out the couples—those who are romantically involved. Or turn the sound down on the TV and watch two teams after a big game. Can you tell the winners from the losers? Our actions and expressions let others know how we are feeling, what we are thinking, and sometimes what we are going to do next.

This is all part of nonverbal communication. In fact, experts say that up to 90 percent of your communication is nonverbal.

Exercise #58

From the feelings list in Section 2, choose a feeling to act out for your small group. The person who first guesses the feeling correctly becomes the next actor. Do this until everyone has acted at least three or four times. In the table below, describe the actor's expressions and movements in the first column. Write down your guess of the feeling in the second column. Then, when the actor tells the correct answer, write the feeling in the third column.

Description	My Guess	Feeling Portrayed

Description	My Guess	Feeling Portrayed

Putting It Together

In your small groups, discuss these questions:

▼ How hard was it to express a feeling to others?

▼ Did some people do better than others at acting out the feelings?

▼ Did some people do better at guessing?

▼ What kinds of feelings were hardest to understand? Why?

▼ What feelings were the easiest to act out? Why?

▼ Can you control how you express your own feelings?

▼ When might that be valuable?

Activity 59.
Present Your Viewpoint

Challenge

He who wants to persuade should put his trust not in the right argument, but in the right word. The power of sound has always been greater than the power of sense.

—Joseph Conrad

In Exercise #56 you took a stand on certain key issues. In this exercise, you will defend your positions and hear other students defend theirs.

Exercise #59

List here an issue you feel strongly about. This can be a controversial topic or a religious one—anything that is important to you:

_____

_____

▼ Write your opinion in bold letters on a 3″-by-5″ card and tape it to your sleeve.

▼ Walk around the room, reading people's cards and letting them read yours. Find three or four other people who feel as you do about your issue.

▼ Assemble the people who hold similar views into a think tank. Prepare to present your viewpoint to the class.

In the space below write an outline for your presentation. What points do you want to make? What questions do you want to answer? What arguments do you anticipate?

_____

_____

_____

_____

List the materials, facts, figures, or illustrations that you need for your presentation:

_____

_____

_____

_____

List who is to do what:

_____

_____

_____

_____

Putting It Together

In your group, discuss these questions:

▼ How did your feelings about the issues change as you worked together with others?

▼ Do others feel more strongly about important issues than you do? Which issues?

▼ What are the advantages and disadvantages of taking strong stands?

▼ When are concepts like *waiting, moderation, acceptance,* and *taking it easy* important?

▼ When is it more appropriate to *jump right in, take a stand,* and *be bold*?

Finally, each group should make its presentation to the entire class.

Activity 60.
Compare with High Standards

Challenge

Write a short article (one page) expressing your opinion. Then find an article by someone who agrees with your opinion. (You can look in magazines, books, research journals, etc.)

Exercise #60

List specific ways your opinion agrees with the published work:

_____

_____

_____

List specific ways your opinion disagrees with the published work:

_____

_____

_____

How would you judge whether an article is good or bad? Create five of your own standards that you would look for in a good article (for example, clarity, consistency, logic):

_____

_____

_____

_____

What rating do you give the published work (check one)?

❏ Excellent   ❏ Good   ❏ Fair   ❏ Poor

What rating do you give your own work (check one)?

❏ Excellent   ❏ Good   ❏ Fair   ❏ Poor

Putting It Together

Work with your small group to make a checklist of things to look for in an article. Share with other groups to come up with a master list of "Qualities of a Good Article."

Have two other people in your group read your article, and use the master list to evaluate it.

When everyone has had an article read by two other people, discuss these questions:

▼ If you didn't do as well as you thought you could, what could you do to improve?

▼ Where can you find help in putting together an article?

Give one another concrete, constructive suggestions for improving your articles.

Activity 61.
My Place

Challenge

Fantasies are more than substitutes for unpleasant reality; they are also dress rehearsals, plans. All acts performed in the world begin in the imagination.

—*Barbara Grizzuti Harrison*

Your eyes are half closed … you are very comfortable as you sit in your chair … feel your body relaxing. Imagine yourself being in your own place—your own piece of the world. It can be a place you have been to … or it can be a place where you would like to be. Relax and allow your thoughts to wander freely.

Exercise #61

Think about what you have just read; and as you relax, think about how you feel.

Now that you are relaxed, where are you? Describe it.

_____

_____

_____

Do you hear anything?

_____

_____

Describe the feeling of the air around you.

_____

_____

What are you doing in this place?

_____

_____

What feelings do you have?

_____

_____

Is there anyone around you?

_____

_____

What are they saying? Doing?

_____

_____

Allow those people to see you and like you. What happens?

_____

_____

 # Putting It Together

Share with your small group what you have imagined. Discuss the following questions:

▼ Is the place you imagined someplace you have been before, or someplace you have only heard about?

▼ Is it a real place, or an imagined one?

▼ Is there a real place in your life that is "your place"?

▼ What role does your place play in your life?

Activity 62.
Curiosity

Challenge

I think, at a child's birth, if a mother could ask a fairy godmother to endow it with the most useful gift, that gift would be curiosity.

—Eleanor Roosevelt

We never stop investigating. We are never satisfied that we know enough to get by. Every question we answer leads on to another question. This has become the greatest survival trick of our species.

—Desmond Morris

You may have heard the expression "Curiosity killed the cat." Curiosity is a hallmark of cats and of humans. We are inherently curious beings. If we weren't curious, the first Americans would never have crossed the Siberian land bridge thousands of years ago, Columbus wouldn't have sailed the Atlantic, and men would never have set foot on the moon.

Our curiosity leads to great discoveries and life-altering changes. Sometimes it leads to disaster. And sometimes it's just plain fun. In this exercise, we'll go for the fun.

Exercise #62

This exercise is to be completed as a class. You'll need the following items:

1. a shoe box with a lid

2. a 5"-by-7" blank or lined card

3. two identical pictures, one of them small enough to fit inside the shoe box

4. a wide-tipped felt marker

Paste one picture inside the end of the shoe box, then tape the lid onto the box. Poke a few holes in the lid to let in light, and make a viewing hole in the other end of the box. Label the hole "Look Here." Use the marker to label the card like this:

```
Look inside!
This is really something!
Don't tell anyone!
```

Now label the box "Peeker Box" and place it where it can be seen by people who are not in your class (for example, in the hallway outside your class door). Stand the card next to the box and tape the duplicate picture on a wall above the box.

Observe and record the number of "peekers" and their reactions. Interview some of the people who stop to look.

Which picture attracted the most viewers? _____

_____

Why did it get more attention? _____

_____

Why is it more inviting to peek? _____

_____

Describe "curiosity." _____

_____

Who was the most curious? _____

_____

Who was the least? _____

_____

Putting It Together

Work with your small group to write a few paragraphs on how *curiosity* relates to *learning*. How is it different? How is it the same? Does one lead to the other, and vice versa? Is one "better" than the other? Use reference books and other resources to find definitions and examples of each.

Activity 63.
Cliff-Hangers

Challenge

The rail around the observation deck broke suddenly, and the man who had been leaning against it plunged from the top of the 100-story building. Halfway down, he hollered to the window washer, "So far, so good!"

What is a *cliff-hanger*? It's a gimmick used by writers to make their audience eager for the sequel to a book, movie, or TV show. At the end of *The Empire Strikes Back*, for example, Han Solo is in the custody of the bounty hunter, and Luke and Leia pledge to rescue him. Will they? You have to see the sequel to find out.

Cliff-hangers are common in the season-ending episodes of TV shows, as well. The writers want to ensure that viewers will come back to the program in September. The term itself comes from the old Saturday matinee movies, when the hero or heroine would be left at the end of the movie, literally hanging from a cliff.

Exercise #63

In your small groups, you will decide on a simple but exciting idea you can expand into an outline for a play.

First, you'll need to decide on the setting. Here are a few ideas to get you started. You can use one of these, or come up with your own:

▼ a stormy night	▼ a misty graveyard
▼ a haunted mansion	▼ a dark forest
▼ a blizzard	▼ a sailboat on the ocean
▼ a cabin at the base of a volcano	▼ a deserted island

Now you need a cast of characters. Here are a few "stock" characters. Again, you can use one or more of them, or come up with your own:

▼ an innocent young girl	▼ a dashing pilot
▼ a sinister-looking scientist	▼ a worldly older woman

▼ a brash young man

▼ a crusty old boat captain

▼ a flashy movie actress

▼ a dark, mysterious stranger

▼ a pipe-smoking detective

▼ a wealthy, eccentric old lady

Finally, you need a plot. One standard plot line gathers several strangers together in an unfamiliar setting, then puts them in danger. They must decide who among them is friend and who is foe. There are countless variations on this theme. You can use one of them, or come up with a new plot all your own.

Use the space below to record your setting, characters, and plot ideas. Brainstorm in your group to come up with new ideas.

Settings	Characters	Plots

As a group, write a two- or three-page skit in which the thrilling conclusion ends prematurely—the reader is left hanging.

Putting It Together

Each group will read or perform its cliff-hanger for the rest of the class.

The class can then assemble the cliff-hangers into a book and print them out. Be creative with this. If you have access to a desktop publishing system, add illustration and design.

Activity 64.
You Decide

Challenge

What would you do if you were suddenly given the ability to make people's lives turn out as you wished?

Have you ever found yourself wishing you could change someone's life? The wish to help others (or to exact revenge) is a natural human trait. In this exercise, you'll get the chance to choose the outcome of three scenarios.

Exercise #64

Read each scenario; then write in the conclusion.

Case Study

Jim decides he needs to be making money by the time he is 18. His family is facing financial pressures, and Jim wants to help out. He looks at all the options available to him at local schools. He needs to have marketable skills, or he will have to work at common labor jobs for less money. He decides to:

_____

_____

_____

_____

Case Study

Alice has always wanted to work with blind children. She is now finishing high school and must decide on future training. Alice feels she cannot wait until she completes college to start working, but she knows a good education will open more doors for her. After much thinking and talking with advisors, she decides to:

_____

_____

_____

_____

Case Study

Dave is very intelligent, and he loves math and working with numbers. He is also very good with his hands—especially at repairing machines. He cannot afford college and he doesn't like sitting in a classroom for four hours or more. After much thought and talking with others, he chooses to:

_____

_____

_____

_____

Putting It Together

Discuss with your small group your story endings and whether you felt a sense of power as you made decisions about someone else's life. Share selected stories with the total group and discuss these questions:

▼ How did you like having the power to give people's lives the endings you wanted?

▼ Are there times in real life when you have that kind of power? When?

▼ Do you ever feel as if someone else has that kind of power over your life? Who?

Activity 65.
What Did People Do Before Reading?

─ Challenge ─

We live in a sensory environment totally different from that of preliterate man—simply because we have learned to read. In shifting from speech to writing, man gave up an ear for an eye, and transferred his interest from spiritual to spatial, from reverential to referential.

—Edmund Carpenter

Exercise #65

Put this paragraph into your own words.

_____

_____

_____

What are some disadvantages of experiencing life in a reading-oriented culture?

_____

_____

What would your personal thoughts be like if the world hadn't discovered reading?

_____

_____

_____

Putting It Together

Share your ideas with others in your group. Decide if reading has enriched or hindered life in general. Discuss the following questions:

▼ What are the advantages of living in a literate world?

▼ What would be the advantages of living in a world where your life depended on perceptions rather than on book-learned knowledge?

▼ What did people do for fun before reading?

▼ What forms of government are most likely among people who cannot read?

Activity 66.

Roots

Challenge

There is the fear, common to all English-only speakers, that the chief purpose of foreign languages is to make fun of us. Otherwise, you know, why not just come out and say it?

—*Barbara Ehrenreich*

Your language is really the sum total of the languages of all of your ancestors, and most words in the English language evolved from hundreds or thousands of years ago. At one point in history, all peoples probably lived together on one huge continent. As each went in different directions, so did the variations of our language.

Exercise #66

Check your library for dictionaries in the languages listed below (or others). Look up the words "man" and "woman" in the dictionaries you find. Then look up the words "mother" and "father." Which words are similar in some languages, and which are different? If you or someone you know speaks a different language, include these too.

▼ French

▼ German

▼ Japanese

▼ Spanish

▼ Swahili

▼ Russian

Work with your team to develop a list of words that describe a successful person. Look up those words in all the foreign-language dictionaries you can find.

English Word	Foreign Translation
_____	_____
_____	_____
_____	_____
_____	_____
_____	_____
_____	_____
_____	_____

Putting It Together

Do you know someone who speaks a language that does not appear on the list above? Find words in that language that are the same (or similar) to words you have looked up in this exercise. Share with your group what you discover.

In your groups, discuss these questions:

▼ Do we know ourselves only by comparing ourselves with others?

▼ How can differences in language cause problems in a democracy?

▼ How can these differences be viewed as strengths?

Activity 67.
Fine Blends

Challenge

Fortunately, the time has long passed when people liked to regard the United States as some kind of melting pot, taking men and women from every part of the world and converting them into standardized, homogenized Americans. We are, I think, much more mature and wise today. Just as we welcome a world of diversity, so we glory in an America of diversity—an America all the richer for the many different and distinctive strands of which it is woven.

—Hubert H. Humphrey

Our flag is red, white and blue, but our nation is a rainbow—red, yellow, brown, black and white—and we're all precious in God's sight.

—Jesse Jackson

Very few people are "native Americans." Even Native Americans (or American Indians) must trace their roots to other continents. Do you know where your family came from?

Many of us today don't remember where our families came from, or when they arrived in the United States. Most of us grow up speaking English; sometimes we even forget that others in the world *don't* speak English. Or we insist they must speak English only when they are in this country.

But English itself is derived from other languages, just like the population of this country is derived from all over the world. In this exercise, you'll explore where your family came from—and where the English language came from, as well.

Exercise #67

How did your ancestors come to the United States? When and why did they come? To find out where your family came from, talk to your parents or grandparents or great aunts and uncles.

Can your relatives remember when someone in your family spoke another language?

_____

_____

_____

When did that person begin speaking English?

_____

_____

Find a language your ancestors spoke. Read about the language and research its roots.

The language: _____

Its roots: _____

Now trace the roots of the English language. Diagram how far it goes back to a common tongue. What other languages developed from the same root? Use a dictionary to find the roots of several English words. Ask your reference librarian for help if you get stuck.

Putting It Together

Get together with others in your class who have ancestors from the same part of the world that your family came from. Prepare a short talk about your heritage for the rest of the class. Include music and photographs, costumes, tools, instruments, and other visual aids, if you can find them.

Activity 68.
Simplify the Complex

Challenge

Cultivators of the Oriental Persimmon propagate the plant by grafting it onto rootstock. The seedling develops a long tap root; but the roots "sucker" prolifically. Seeds require stratification in moist peat.

What makes for good, clean writing? Do you recognize it when you see it? Can you define it? Can you produce it? In this exercise, you'll get a chance to try.

Exercise #68

1. Rewrite the *Challenge* paragraph above so that it would make sense to a third-grader, yet doesn't change the meaning.

_____

_____

_____

2. Now work with one or two partners to rewrite an article from a popular science magazine. (Use separate sheets of paper for this.) Write it for a third-grade class, simplifying the graphics. Make sure you use all the information. Create, give, and grade short pre- and post-tests to see whether the class understood the presentation.

3. Use sketches to simplify the following ideas (practice on scratch paper first).

a household appliance

a lunar-type landing system

a bicycle

a mousetrap

Putting It Together

Each member of your small group should write a paragraph about him- or herself, using clean, simple language. When you have all finished, each member should read his or her paragraph out loud. Make suggestions to one another on making the paragraphs simpler, easier, and more straightforward.

Activity 69.

Complicate the Simple

Challenge

I know not, Madam, that you have a right, upon moral principles, to make your readers suffer so much.

—*Samuel Johnson*

Why would anyone want to write to confuse people? Yet the courts and colleges and insurance companies seem to be filled with such writers. In this exercise, you'll try your hand at *obfuscation*—the art of making the simple complex.

Exercise #69

1. Rewrite the following paragraph to "stretch the brain" of a college senior:

   The best learning takes place when your mind is relaxed, open, and interested.

   _____

   _____

   _____

   _____

   _____

2. Work with one or two partners to rewrite an article or story from a first- to third-grade book. Write it at the level of a senior high school class. Keep the information intact, yet make it interesting to the class. Create, give, and grade short pre- and post-tests to see whether the class grasps the content of the presentation.

3. Use sketches to complicate the following items (practice on scratch paper first).

a household appliance

a lunar-type landing system

a bicycle

a mousetrap

Putting It Together

Each member of your small group should write a paragraph about him- or herself, using complicated, fussy language. When you have all finished, each member should read his or her paragraph out loud. Make suggestions to one another on making the paragraphs more complex, wordy, and difficult.

Activity 70.
Illusions

Challenge

Don't part with your illusions. When they are gone you may still exist, but you have ceased to live.

—*Mark Twain*

What is an illusion? The dictionary defines the word this way: **a.** An erroneous perception of reality. **b.** An erroneous concept or belief.

In exercise #70, you have been hired by an illusionist to write short descriptions of his optical illusions.

Exercise #70

Write one or two short sentences to describe each illusion below. Practice what you say out loud; then write it on a separate sheet of paper. Say it clearly but briefly. You may label or number lines, angles, or circles to assist in your description. When you are satisfied with your descriptions, copy them into this book.

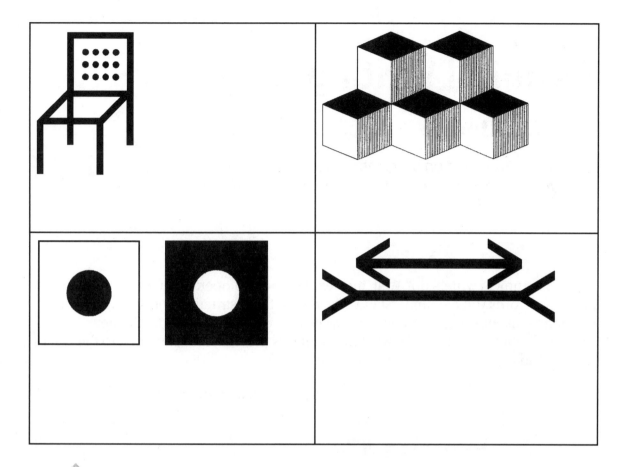

Putting It Together

"What am I doing here?" you may be thinking about now. "This author must be totally nuts. When in my life will I *ever* have to describe illusions?"

Share your descriptions with your small group. Get and give suggestions. Discuss the following questions:

▼ What value is there in this exercise?

▼ Is this exercise good practice for anything useful?

▼ What do technical writers do?

Activity 71.
Technical Writing

Challenge

Today the function of the artist is to bring imagination to science and science to imagination, where they meet, in the myth.

—Cyril Connolly

What do technical writers do? Well, they explain how to operate the computer you just bought, in words you can understand. They write the instructions on setting up the new coffee maker, on assembling the new furniture, and on installing the new software. Technical writers take what the scientists provide, and explain it to the rest of the world so that the rest of the world can use it.

In this exercise, you will get a taste of what the technical writer does.

Exercise #71

Explain and describe the following illustrations.

Describe how this Scale-o-brator works. Invent terms and parts.

_____

_____

_____

_____

_____

_____

_____

_____

Explain how to fly this glider.

JOYSTICK

FOOT
PEDALS

RS23g

_____

_____

_____

_____

_____

_____

_____

How do you play this game? Give it a name.

_____

_____

_____

_____

_____

_____

Tell how to build this triangle.

_____

_____

_____

_____

_____

_____

Describe how to go down the stairs.

_____

_____

_____

_____

_____

Explain the advantage of this "pair" of scissors.

_____

_____

_____

_____

_____

_____

Putting It Together

In your small groups, read one another's descriptions and discuss the following questions:

▼ What is the most important thing about giving directions to someone else?

▼ Could you have been more precise in your directions for this exercise?

The next time you bring home a product with instructions, read through them and ask yourself, "How could the writer have made these instructions clearer?"

Activity 72.
Alike and Different

— **Challenge** —————————

All this talk about equality. The only thing people really have in common is that they are all going to die.

—*Bob Dylan*

Have you heard the expression, "That's like comparing apples and oranges"? People say it when they're telling you two items are too different to be compared. But, when you think about it, apples and oranges have a lot in common. They're both fruits. They both have peels. They both are sweet. They both grow on trees. And people like to eat them. Bob Dylan notwithstanding, you can find similarities in a host of things that look very different at first glance.

In this exercise, you will be describing differences and similarities, not between two sets of things, but within one set.

Exercise #72

Instead of looking for the differences between two different objects, find a similarity and a difference between each of the following groups of items:

Group	Similarities	Differences
Toasters	have heating elements	some toast 2 slices some toast 4 or more
Families		
Motivated students		
Aggressive people		

I AM *ALREADY* SUCCESSFUL

Group	Similarities	Differences
Creative persons		
Methods of transportation		
Wars		
Ecosystems		
Political systems		
Loving people		

Putting It Together

Share your answers with others in your group. As a group, list ways you are similar to and different from one another. How are you similar to and different from students in China? In Brazil? In Russia?

174 I AM *ALREADY* SUCCESSFUL

Activity 73.
Your Page

Challenge

Solitude begets whimsies.

—*Lady Mary Wortley Montagu*

You have 15 minutes to yourself on this page.

Putting It Together

Share your page with your small group and discuss these questions:

▼ Did 15 minutes of silence feel comfortable to you? Or were you nervous?

▼ Do you like have time on your own?

▼ Are you more comfortable in the company of others?

Activity 74.
Thoughts and Feelings

Challenge

My advice to people today is as follows: If you take the game of life seriously, if you take your nervous system seriously, if you take your sense organs seriously, if you take the energy process seriously, you must turn on, tune in, and drop out.

—Timothy Leary

You can tune in to your perceptions and feelings right now—at this very moment.

Exercise #74

In the spaces below, record your answers to the following questions.

▼ *Right now*—What do you see and hear (what are your eyes and ears experiencing) at this moment?

_____

_____

_____

_____

▼ *Right now*—What are you thinking (what messages are in your head) at this moment?

_____

_____

_____

_____

▼ *Right now*—What do you feel (what is going on in your whole body) at this moment?

_____

_____

_____

_____

Putting It Together

Share your *nows* with other members of your small group. How are their *nows* different? How are they similar?

Discuss the following questions:

▼ Are there times when you confuse your thoughts with your feelings?

▼ How can you separate your thoughts from your feelings?

▼ When is it important to do that?

▼ When is it hardest to do that?

Activity 75.
Who You Were

Challenge

How simple a thing it seems to me that to know ourselves as we are, we must know our mothers' names.

—*Alice Walker*

You are the result of all the people and factors that influence your life. You are the child of your parents, who were the children of their parents. Besides all that, you have learned behaviors that have become part of you that have little do to with your parents.

So, you are the sum total of your heredity and your learned behavior—and you are *more than that*. You are a person who is different from anyone ever born. You are everything that has shaped you and more.

Exercise #75

List three things you do just like your parents. Do you walk the same way your father does, or sneeze as loudly as your grandfather? Do you laugh like your mother?

1. _____

2. _____

3. _____

List three ways you have influenced your parents or changed their lives. (If you don't know, ask them.)

1. _____

2. _____

3. _____

What did your parents want to be when they were your age?

_____

_____

_____

Putting It Together

In your small group, discuss the following questions:

▼ Who is responsible for your being who you are?

▼ How do you respond to that person?

▼ What makes you different from your parents?

Activity 76.
Who You Are

Challenge

Do I contradict myself?
Very well then I contradict myself,
(I am large, I contain multitudes).

—*Walt Whitman*

You are different today from who you were yesterday. You are not the same as you were an hour ago. You are changing all the time. Even your body cells are dying and being replaced at the rate of thousands per minute. Who you are can accurately be stated only at this very moment in time. You are a changing, dynamic individual— different from all others.

Exercise #76

Change is not always easy, but it is a fact of life. As you answer the questions below, try to think of change as a positive, healthy process. Not something to be feared, but something to embrace.

List three ways you are different today from the way you were a year ago:

1. _____

2. _____

3. _____

List three ways you are the same as you were a year ago:

1. _____

2. _____

3. _____

List three things about yourself that have remained constant as long as you can remember:

1. _____

2. _____

3. _____

Putting It Together

Discuss the changes and differences in you with your group. Discuss the following questions:

▼ Are you different now from who *you expected to be* a year ago?

▼ Are changes in your life occurring fast enough?

▼ Are they occurring too fast?

▼ Who is in control of who you become?

Activity 77.
Who You Will Be

Challenge

Every moment of one's existence one is growing into more or retreating into less. One is always living a little more or dying a little bit.

—*Norman Mailer*

Tomorrow you will be different from who you are today. The change may be small and hardly noticeable—but you will change.

In some ways, you change naturally, without conscious decision. But some situations force you to use rational thinking and imagination to change. You are always becoming *you*.

Exercise #77

Again, try to think of change as a healthy, natural process. Whether we like it or not, we will change continually.

List three ways you change naturally:

1. _____

2. _____

3. _____

List three ways that change can be forced upon you:

1. _____

2. _____

3. _____

List three places in your life where you need to change:

1. _____

2. _____

3. _____

Putting It Together

In your small group, discuss the changes in your life that have occurred naturally or by choice. Discuss the following questions:

▼ Is it easier to change by choice or by necessity?

▼ Are there people in your life who seem never to change?

▼ How might those people be changing?

Activity 78.

You Were, Are, and Will Be ...

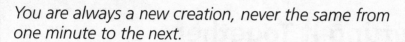

Challenge

You are always a new creation, never the same from one minute to the next.

Take a few minutes and think about what you have learned about yourself in this book. Flip back through the pages and read through some of your answers. Are there surprises in some of your answers? Would you answer some of the questions in Section 1 differently today than you did before?

Exercise #78

Write down your thoughts about yourself as you were, as you are now, and as you imagine you will be.

I was: _____

_____

_____

_____

_____

I am: _____

_____

_____

_____

_____

I will be: _____

_____

_____

_____

_____

Putting It Together

In your small group, read your thoughts aloud to one another. Discuss the following questions:

▼ If we are always changing, what part of us stays constant?

▼ Is there a core inside us that does not change?

▼ How do your relationships with others change if you and they are always changing?

Activity 79.

Seeds of Service 3

Challenge

Though language forms the preacher,
'Tis "good works" make the man.

—*Eliza Cook*

Once again, you have the opportunity to think about what you have to give, rather than about what you can get.

Exercise #79

As a class, brainstorm a list of ways you can serve others by giving of yourselves. Write these ideas down in the space below so that you'll have the list to refer back to later.

_____

_____

_____

_____

_____

_____

_____

_____

_____

_____

_____

Putting It Together

As a whole class, discuss the meaning of the word *service*. Have any of you started putting your seeds of service into action?

Make the following resolutions to yourself:

▼ I will look over these seeds of service every now and then.

▼ I will watch for how these ideas begin to influence my activities, hobbies, career choices, service to the world, friendships, and spiritual values.

▼ I will make a difference in the world.

Activity 80.
Time Capsule Revisited

Challenge

When I die, my epitaph should read: She Paid the Bills.
That's the story of my private life.

—Gloria Swanson

In Section 1 of this book, you were asked to write down important things about yourself to be placed in a time capsule to be opened in 100 years. Now let's assume that NASA has had a problem with its capsule program, and it has not yet been launched. You have the opportunity now to rewrite your program for the time capsule.

Exercise #80

Completely rewrite your program for the time capsule. Use what you have discovered about yourself in this book.

_____

_____

_____

_____

_____

_____

Putting It Together

Share your capsule narrative with your small group. Discuss these questions:

▼ What is different about your time capsule entry? How have you changed?

▼ Is anyone's entry the same from the beginning of the year?

Simulation 3.
The Communiqué

In Simulations 1 and 2, you used your creativity and understanding of yourself to include others in your "circle of importance." You learned that feeling successful is an attitude that includes acceptance of who and what you *already* are. You also saw that your success requires dealing with other people. You used these skills to create *The Game* and *The Business* in previous simulations.

In this third simulation, *The Communiqué*, you will communicate to the world. You also will think about what you can do to serve the world. Language has been your tool to learn more about yourself. Now you will use language to share.

Creating *The Communiqué*

Your group has expanded to merge all the teams into one, large corporation dedicated to helping the world. You have decided to assist in public education, human rights, health and welfare, ecology, and other sensitive areas.

Meet as teams to discuss your commitment to the issues. Representatives from your group will coordinate with other teams' representatives to discuss and plan the corporation newsletter, *The Communiqué*. This newsletter will present information, views, opinions, prospective programs, projections, and anything else you want to include. (These meetings will be conducted with all members of the simulation teams.)

The newsletter represents the organization and will become the model for a quarterly publication. Your task is to take the simulation from the first, unpolished ideas and assignment of responsibilities to an actual finished product.

First you must fill the following positions:

▼ Managing Editor(s)

▼ Writers

▼ Designers

▼ Photographers

▼ Typesetters

▼ Advertising People

▼ Printers

▼ Distributors

▼ Others

▼ _____

▼ _____

▼ _____

▼ _____

Do what is necessary to make the product. Devise periodic evaluations to see how the simulation is going.

If you are frustrated, bored, or out of touch, meet with the assignment team to reflect, discuss, and make the project a satisfying process for you. *You* must assume the responsibility for making it work for you. Help your coworkers stay on track.

Evaluating Your Progress

List the problems you encountered and their solutions.

Problem	Solution

Congratulations! You have completed the newsletter. Evaluate *The Communiqué* according to the criteria for good writing you created in Exercise #60. Then evaluate your progress and the progress of the people in your groups.

Small Group Inventory 3

Now that you have completed the last simulation in this book, think carefully about how your group worked together. Fill out this inventory individually.

Characteristic	Low	Average	High
1. Level of sincerity			
You all tried to do your best	1	2	3
You all attempted to learn more	1	2	3
Comments			
2. Research			
Used many sources	1	2	3
Clear, straightforward sharing of material	1	2	3
Comments			
3. Awareness			
You attempted to listen to the ideas of others	1	2	3
Level at which the group communicates ideas	1	2	3
Comments			
4. Cooperation			
Level at which you worked together	1	2	3
You tried to understand the needs of others	1	2	3
Comments			

Characteristic	Low	Average	High
5. Product			
You completed your work	1	2	3
Clarity of work	1	2	3
Appearance of work	1	2	3
Comments			
6. Your Overall Satisfaction with the Group	1	2	3
Comments			

Self-Inventory 3

Now evaluate yourself. How are you doing so far? Before you begin answering these questions, review your responses in Sections 1 and 2 and what you have learned about yourself.

Ask yourself these questions honestly and with a fair degree of self-examination.

Characteristic	Low	Average	High
1. My Level of Sincerity			
I desired to do my best	1	2	3
I attempted to learn more	1	2	3
I tried to cooperate	1	2	3
2. My Research			
I used many sources	1	2	3
I wrote clear, straightforward responses in book	1	2	3
I tried to find more resources	1	2	3

Characteristic	Low	Average	High
3. My Awareness of Myself			
I discovered new things	1	2	3
I tried to improve	1	2	3
I worked on personal challenges	1	2	3
4. My Awareness of Others			
I cooperated in my group	1	2	3
Level of my ability to communicate ideas	1	2	3
My ability to assist others	1	2	3
5. My Written and Oral Product			
Quality of my oral report	1	2	3
Excellence of my written work	1	2	3
Amount of preparation for oral or written work	1	2	3
6. Carryover Outside School			
Homework	1	2	3
Degree of interest in my studies	1	2	3
Hobbies and interests that relate to this course	1	2	3
7. My Overall Sense of Personal Satisfaction			
My satisfaction with my personal growth	1	2	3
My ability to be a friend	1	2	3
My awareness of the world	1	2	3
Amount of available energy I used	1	2	3
Degree I progressed compared to my potential	1	2	3

You Are Successful: Some Final Thoughts

You are a different person from who you were when you began this book. Your brain cells have made a complete change, your attitude is better, and you interact and communicate more effectively with other people.

List four major things you have learned about yourself:

1. _____

2. _____

3. _____

4. _____

List what you have learned about your communication skills:

_____

_____

Describe how you can better serve the world:

_____

_____

Congratulations!

In *The Wizard of Oz* the Tin Man thought he needed a heart—but all he needed was a ticking pocket watch and confidence. The Straw Man thought he needed a brain—but all he needed was a diploma and recognition. The Lion thought he needed courage—but all he needed was a medal and someone to believe in him.

Each character learned that he was already successful. Each just needed official recognition of qualities that were already there.

This is your official recognition.

Congratulations! You are already successful!

I am *Already* **Successful**

This is official recognition of

_____

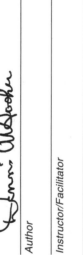

Who has completed the program "I Am Already Successful"
and has the rights and privileges given to all persons who
consider themselves *Already Successful*.

Signed _____
        Author

Signed _____
        Instructor/Facilitator

Date _____

NOTES

NOTES

NOTES

NOTES

NOTES

NOTES